# SOUL WARRIOR

## Accessing Realms Beyond the Veil

## HOUSE OF INDIGO

# Disclaimer

The publisher and the author are providing this book and its contents on an "as is" basis and make no representations or warranties of any kind with respect to this book or its contents. The publisher and the author disclaim all such representations and warranties, including but not limited to warranties of healthcare for a particular purpose. In addition, the publisher and the author assume no responsibility for errors, inaccuracies, omissions, or any other inconsistencies herein.

The content of this book is for informational purposes only and is not intended to diagnose, treat, cure, or prevent any condition or disease. You understand that this book is not intended as a substitute for consultation with a licensed practitioner. Please consult with your own physician or healthcare specialist regarding the suggestions and recommendations made in this book. The use of this book implies your acceptance of this disclaimer.

The publisher and the author make no guarantees concerning the level of success you may experience by following the advice and strategies contained in this book, and you accept the risk that results will differ for each individual. The testimonials and examples provided in this book show exceptional results, which may not apply to the average reader, and are not intended to represent or guarantee that you will achieve the same or similar results.

# Contents

# Introduction

In Soul Warrior: Accessing Realms Beyond the Veil, you will be introduced to the courageous leaders who have stepped forward to share stories of the soul, the journey each has been on in becoming a warrior and how it has changed their life experience.

What does it take to become a soul warrior? What does one need to endure or experience? What initiations have occurred to mold us into the psychics, healers and coaches we are?

A Dark Night of the Soul, awakening, returning to familial gifts, connecting to nature, fairies, the akashic records, ancient traditions, energetic healing, subconscious work, connecting with spirit, wisdom and deep internal guidance, are some of the ways these women have accessed and connected with the spiritual, energetic and subconscious realms to support themselves and their clients.

Mostly, these experiences change the entire fabric of our lives. Yet, the author's souls are that of a warrior, and continue on their mission as they are faced with challenges, overcoming them time and again.

As we learn to pierce the veil, the gifts, the magic and the mystery are awaiting us. Our lives are forever changed as we willingly walk through our shadows, fears and illusions for the betterment of all.

Won't you join us?

Jessica Verrill
Founder, House of Indigo

# ONE

## Pamala Oslie

### MESSAGES FROM "THE OTHER SIDE"

As a Psychic Medium, I have been talking with guides and people's loved ones on the other side for decades. These are just some of the insights and messages I've received from these loving Beings. This information includes a grander and more expansive understanding of ourselves and the nature of reality.

Here are some of the fascinating topics those on "the other side" have shared:

## Change is Happening

Most of us sense there is a shift happening – something feels different about our lives and the world. It can look and feel like life is falling apart, which is creating fear and panic in many people. Our old sense of security and stability is disintegrating; our familiar systems are collapsing all around us. Even the weather seems to be getting into the act – unpredictable, destructive, uncontrollable, and scary.

There are always multiple perspectives – many ways we could see what is happening. We could take the optimistic and hopeful perspective that our souls know what they're doing and are forcing us to evolve, or we could take the fearful, pessimistic view that we are greedy, unconscious, and selfish humans doomed to extinction.

Fortunately, guides have been emphasizing positive perspectives and outcomes. When the caterpillar is transitioning into a butterfly, it starts to fall apart, and parts begin to die off. This is something that happens to allow the butterfly to emerge. It's doubtful that the caterpillar experiences fear or anxiety around this metamorphosis. It intuitively or instinctively knows this is part of its journey to some other, more expansive life experience.

If we can become still and quiet our minds, our intuition would tell us something grand is occurring. What is happening now is not merely a physical wake-up call – a sign that we need to treat the planet better or stop wars, starvation, and injustice. We are experiencing something bigger and much more profound.

What we now have the opportunity to do – what we're ultimately forcing ourselves to do – is to shift our thinking, to have a different understanding of life, ourselves, and our understanding of "reality." We now have the opportunity to evolve our consciousness.

One of the beliefs that causes trouble here is our belief that we are limited, physical beings who live in a finite world, one of scarcity and lack, and that there is only so much to go around, so we must fight to get what we can and struggle to survive.

What Beings on the other side are sharing instead is that we are boundless, unlimited beings; we are masters of our own destinies. There is something magical and mysterious about who we are, something grand and magnificent. We create our own experiences through the power of our thoughts, feelings, and beliefs. Our ability to create what we want is limited only by our imagination and by the belief that we are limited.

If we understand that our thoughts, feelings, and beliefs create our experiences, we can choose to create everything we have always wanted and more. We can dramatically change our experiences and our world.

Special side note: Not only are Beings on the other side sharing this intriguing information about how much more expansive and powerful we truly are, but quantum physics is confirming this profound information too.

We've been living an old paradigm or belief system that says we, and the entire universe, are biological and physical machines that exist for a brief time, then eventually suffer entropy, disintegration, and death.

However, quantum physics has discovered that "reality" and everything is just energy; that matter is not solid at all. All that exists is energy, a field of infinite possibilities.

Quantum physicists are also finding evidence to show that our consciousness affects this energy. There are waves of information and infinite possibilities until an observer focuses attention on the field. Then particles blink into existence.

In alignment with this revelation, these are some of the teachings that Beings on the other side are sharing:

1) We are powerful beings with no limits to what we can create. We have an inherent ability to create our experience through the power of our beliefs, thoughts, and feelings.

2) We have free will. We can choose our beliefs and change our reality; we can create whatever we desire.

3) We limit our ability to create what we desire by limiting our perceptions of what is possible. If we repeatedly affirm our belief in limitations, we will continue to experience that. As we begin to affirm that we are unlimited, we begin to perceive and experience new freedom.

Everything in our lives originates within us. We create or draw to us every experience and person that exists in our lives. This idea can frighten or upset many of us until we discover the real freedom and power that lies within it. By knowing that we are the creators of our experience, we also come to realize that we can change our experiences if we aren't happy with our creations.

Life is a creative adventure. It's your choice to believe whatever you want to believe. We do, however, make life tougher on ourselves when we accept limiting, self-defeating, and self-critical beliefs.

## Why are we here?

We've chosen to come to this physical plane for the experience and to expand the IS/All That Is/The Universe. It's similar to the reason we go to the movies – to have adventures, to learn something, and/or to feel emotions. We aren't being punished or karmically paying for something we did in another life. All lives are happening simultaneously, not linearly. There is no time on the other side. So how can you "pay for something" that is just now happening in another lifetime? Your soul is eternal and immortal. Your soul is multi-dimensional. You are not limited to one lifetime, one body, or just one experience in time. Your soul is adventurous and curious and loves to create. What else are you going to do throughout eternity? You chose to come here for the experience.

## Reincarnation

Imagine that you're in a theatrical play, and all the people in the play are playing different characters. You connect with each other in the play, interacting and playing roles within a certain plot and storyline.

Then when the play is over, you go backstage for a while and hang out with the other actors, which now have become good friends because you've all been working in the play together.

Some of you may decide not to act in a play for a while and choose to take a break. So, you hang out backstage until you want to be in another production. (You're hanging out between lives.)

When you decide you want to create another play, you choose the setting, the environment, the time, the era, and the plot for that play. You write the script and create another drama, comedy, horror, or action-adventure. Then other actors who want to be in the same type of play join in. Each actor pretends to be a different character in this play, but you all still know each other. You just pretend that you don't know each other so that the new story is convincing.

Also, it's often the case that someone who is "challenging" you in this lifetime is doing so because, on a soul level, he/she loves you very much and has chosen to play out the bad guy or nemesis for you so you can work something out, or learn something that you wanted to learn or have an experience that you wanted to have because you were curious about how that experience would feel.

Some of your friends/actors join you in the new play; others decide to be in a different play for now. But those actors will join you again in another play at another time - if they're interested in the plot and storyline of the next play. Ultimately you won't forget the other actors because you have an infinite bond with them through your love for each other.

We're fun-loving, curious, creative souls who love to create plays and "movies" and other adventures. We also love to see who we are and what we're capable of creating, overcoming, or enduring, which is why we sometimes choose more challenging roles and "plays". It's amazing what types of "plays" we choose to create - just for the experience, or to learn something, or just to see how it feels.

If you're not enjoying the theater production you're currently in, you have permission to re-write the script - even in the middle of the play. You chose a theme and storyline before you came, but you still have free will to re-write that script. It's more of an "improvisational" play, so you can change things as you go along.

Speaking with many guides and loved ones who have crossed over – this is what life here seems to be about.

The only difference in this analogy is that all these plays are happening at the same time. You're not choosing one play at a time; your soul is creating multiple productions at the same time! That's how expansive and multi-dimensional your soul truly is.

## How the colors in your aura reveal the personality you've chosen to be in this lifetime.

We all emit energy, an aura. Science calls it an electromagnetic field. Even if we can't see this energy, we've all felt it – we've felt instantly comfortable or drawn to someone but uncomfortable around someone else. We're sensing their energy.

Your aura has different colors that reveal important information about what you've chosen to experience in this lifetime - your life theme, personality, priorities, relationship styles, most fulfilling career directions, potential health issues, and more. Learning about your aura colors can help you understand your choices and help you live a happier, more fulfilling life. And learning about the other aura color personalities can help you create more compatible, harmonious, and fulfilling relationships with others.

Most people have a combination of two main aura colors. The two colors can be compatible or potentially create inner conflict. Developing the positive qualities of each aura color can help you live your best life.

## Here are very brief descriptions of the positive qualities of the aura colors.

**Red** – physical, passionate, sensual, strong-willed, hot-tempered

Reds are physical and sexual. They love expressing themselves through their sensuality and their physical bodies. They live their lives with zest, strength, courage, and self-confidence. Reds prefer to experience the physical nature of life.

**Orange** - physical daredevils, thrill-seekers, extreme athletes

Oranges are the thrill-seekers and daredevils of the aura spectrum. They love the challenge and excitement of physical danger. They love to challenge their environment and go beyond limits. Oranges put their lives on the line just to feel alive and to feel a sense of accomplishment and satisfaction. They love the adrenaline rush of excitement in the face of danger. For Oranges, thrills, cunning skill, and excitement are the essentials in life.

**Magenta** - eccentric, outrageous, bizarre, creative, loves to shock people

Magentas are free-spirited, innovative, creative, rebellious outcasts. They enjoy creating bizarre, controversial objects that are artsy, trendy, and shocking. Their imagination knows no limits. They like taking physical substance and twisting it into strange new forms that go beyond what people consider normal.

**Yellow** - fun-loving, humorous, youthful, rebellious, sensitive, creative, healer, or athletic

Yellows are either the most fun-loving, free-spirited, energetic, and childlike personalities in the aura spectrum, or they are shy, introverted, and sensitive pleasers. Yellows are usually optimistic beings whose life purpose is to bring joy to people, to have fun, and/or to help heal others. These playful characters have a great sense of humor. They love to laugh and to make others laugh. They believe life is to be enjoyed.

**Tan** - logical, practical, grounded, works with details & technology, values stability

Tans are logical and analytical. They choose to process every step, from one through ten. They need to analyze and comprehend the logic in each step before proceeding to the next. They like to establish a firm foundation and then slowly build brick by brick, step by step. They are responsible and have the patience to deal with the details. They prefer security and stability and are typically long-term employees.

**Green** – quick, intelligent, ambitious, driven, workaholic, business-minded

Greens are some of the most powerful, intelligent, quick-thinking movers and shakers in the aura spectrum. They are driven to accomplish, to learn, to set goals, and to make money. Usually, Greens are drawn to power, money, and business. These quick thinkers are organized and efficient. They write lists and check off items as they are completed. They can accomplish anything they set their mind on.

**Blue** - emotional, highly spiritual, intuitive, supportive, teachers, counselors, nurses

Blues are loving, nurturing, supportive, and caring givers. They live from their hearts. They are the most emotional of all the aura colors. Their life purpose is to give love, to teach love, and to learn they are loved. Their priorities are love, relationships, and spirituality. They are constantly helping others. They want to make sure everyone feels loved and accepted. People always turn to Blues for comfort and counsel, and the loyal Blues are always there for them.

**Violet** - visionary, leader, global humanitarian, passionate; activists, performers, musicians, teachers, therapists, politicians, lawyers

Violets are the passionate, inspirational visionaries, leaders, entertainers, and teachers who are here to help save the planet. Most Violets feel drawn to educate the masses, to inspire and empower others, to improve the quality of life here, and to make a big contribution to the planet. Violets have an inner sense that their destiny is greater than that of the average person. Most have felt this way since childhood, when they imagined becoming famous, traveling the planet, or joining humanitarian causes.

**Lavender** - daydreamers, sensitive, imaginative

Lavenders are creative, sensitive, loving, kind, and enjoy fantasy, enchantment, dreams, myths, spiritual beings, angels, and fairies. Lavenders enjoy imagining and exploring fantasy worlds. They prefer to spend time out of their bodies, where life is pretty and enchanting. It is challenging for these airy beings to live in three-dimensional reality. They prefer beautiful versions of the world, with butterflies, flowers, and wood nymphs rather than dirt, concrete, and large cities. Physical reality seems cold and harsh to them.

**Crystal** - quiet, intelligent, spiritual, sensitive, easily overwhelmed, healer

Crystals are quiet, intelligent, spiritual, healers who can be over-whelmed by being around too many people. The Crystal's gift is to help people clear blockages so their body's natural healing can occur. Crystals like everything to be pretty, clean, and gentle. Because they like simplicity and cleanliness, their environments tend to be quiet and orderly. Crystals are auric chameleons, often taking on the aura colors of others around them.

**Indigo** - psychic, androgynous, spiritual

Indigos are highly intuitive, psychic, independent, fearless, strong willed, stubborn, honest, aware, advanced, and sensitive. Indigos are advanced souls who know who they are and where they came from. They are typically androgynous. They are so unusual and spiritually advanced that some people find it difficult to know how to deal with them. Indigos are born with their spiritual memories intact. Many parents report that their Indigo children remember past/other lives, can read minds, are psychic, and/or have encounters with spiritual beings.

(Discover your own aura colors at Auracolors.com)

## How to Communicate with the Other Side

You too have the ability to communicate with people, as well as spiritual guides and teachers who are in different realms. We only experience apparent *separation* because we believe in it. We've either been taught that when people die, they cease to exist or that souls go to a realm that is beyond our reach. Many of you, however, have felt your loved ones around you. Trust what you feel.

Some people believe we can't connect with these souls, while others teach that we shouldn't connect with them. I support us going beyond our old limiting, fear-based beliefs. My experience is that guides and people who have crossed over want to connect with loved ones here! Some souls in the other realms show up to reassure their loved ones that they are happy, not alone, no longer in pain, and in a place of peace and joy. Some show up to offer support and guidance to those on this side.

## How to Connect

Believing that life continues and that souls exist in these other realms is paramount to your ability to communicate with them. It's also important to believe this is possible and that you are just as capable of communicating with souls on the other side as you are with those on this side of the veil.

Learning to be still and quieting the mind is helpful when you first begin this process. Subtle information can get lost in an overactive and busy mind.

When you connect with people and guides on the other side, you may first intuitively sense their presence. Many people report feeling physical sensations, such as goosebumps or tingling sensations.

Most loved ones will purposely appear or feel the way you remember them; they usually exhibit the same personality traits that they had when they were in a physical body so you can identify them. Even though they continue to evolve and grow on the other side, they know how to reveal themselves in a way that their loved ones can recognize them. Sometimes souls will show the evolved version of themselves, so be open to that version when you connect with your loved ones.

Most of these souls will share information with you telepathically; they'll send you thoughts, feelings, or visual images. You may *see* these Beings with your inner eye. A vision may show up inside your mind. On a rare occasion, you may see a flash of light or a faint image with your physical eyes. Some people may hear an actual voice. However, it is more common to receive information and visual images telepathically.

The main reason people have difficulty connecting with the other side is because they don't believe they can do it, that others may be able to do it, but they can't. If I can connect with souls and guides on the other side, that means **all** of us have that innate ability.

People may struggle to connect with a loved one because they are emotionally traumatized by their loved one's passing. If you are emotionally distraught, it can be difficult to quiet your mind and get out of your own way so you can hear or feel your loved one trying to connect with you. Give it time. They may visit you in your dreams.

Some people believe they want to connect with the other side, but subconsciously they are afraid, so they prevent the experience. They may fear seeing or experiencing something that disturbs them. Or they fear it could be emotionally difficult to reconnect with those they can no longer touch or hold.

Some fear they could become overwhelmed or worry that once they access this ability, they won't be able to turn it off. This type of fear can limit you. Truthfully, you are a powerful being. You have control over this skill. You can turn it on and off at any time.

You can ask for signs or proof that someone is communicating with you. Sometimes souls will find a way to give you that proof. Just be open to those signs. And usually, you will have a sense of what their message is when you see that sign.

Since most of the time, your loved ones or guides will send you telepathic messages, one of the ways to tell if it's a particular loved one or a guide talking to you is to notice the words and language used.

Loved ones on the other side typically express themselves just as they did on this side so that you can recognize them. And guides often use words that you don't.

Be still, ask, listen for answers, and learn to trust what you hear, see, sense, or feel.

The ability to communicate with guides or loved ones who have left their *physical* bodies can be very comforting. It can reduce suffering and sorrow. It can create healing for those left behind. And it reinforces that we always have a continuous connection and broadens our perception of who we are and our true abilities.

## About the Author

### PAMALA OSLIE

Pamala Oslie is an author, consultant, radio show host, professional psychic intuitive, and aura expert. Pamala has appeared on ABC, CBS, NBC, CNN, FOX, The Dr. Oz Show, The View, The Ricki Lake Show, Coast to Coast with George Noory, Hallmark's Home & Family, Gaiam TV with Lisa Garr, and many other television and radio shows. She has also been featured in many national magazines.

Pam has written four successful and popular books, Life Colors, Love Colors, Infinite You and Make Your Dreams Come True, and has a very extensive clientele, including many celebrities. Pam has spoken at the TEDx Talks, the International Forum on New Science, Fortune 500 companies, and many seminars for professionals in the psychology, education, health fields and more. She was awarded the Holistic Transformational Leader of the Year Award by the Global Association of Holistic Psychotherapy and Coaching.

Pam is the Founder of www.AuraColors.com a site designed to help you create success, joy and fulfillment in EVERY area of your life. She also developed www.LoveColors.com, this site is designed to help you find love and friendships by matching you with people who have compatible aura colors.

Facebook:
https://www.facebook.com/pam.oslie

https://www.facebook.com/auracolors
https://www.facebook.com/LoveColorsAura
https://www.facebook.com/auracolorsireland
Twitter:
https://twitter.com/auracolors
https://twitter.com/LoveColorsAura
https://twitter.com/PamOslie
Instagram:
https://www.instagram.com/pamoslie/

# TWO

## Linda Anzelc Huitt

### THE JOURNEY OF A WAYSHOWER WARRIOR

What am I doing here in this book? *Me??* I used to work for a large insurance company, where some people called me the "spreadsheet queen"…a manager of project managers…a technical coach and business planner—completely driven by facts, data, and logic, and compensated for my problem solving and leadership skills. Yet here I am, sharing my experience about the other side of the veil. *What?? How did that happen?* But that is the journey that Spirit presented to me. And oh how grateful I am! Not just for being where I am now, but for the whole journey. That is what makes me the kind of Soul Warrior that I am—a Lightworker. A Wayshower. And I am here to tell you that you, yes YOU, just might be one too. Anyone can access the support and wisdom from the other side of the veil if they so desire.

Let me give you my quick perspective on what is meant by "the veil". It is simply this–that part of the ethers that is a separation between our physical world, and the non-physical world which extends far beyond the physical. When we work with Angels, pray to our higher powers, or participate in mediumship or psychic read-ings, we are accessing the other side of the veil. Not so mysterious now, right?

## What is a Wayshower?

*"Begin with the end in mind"* – Stephen Covey

If I am going to tell you about my journey, I first need to tell you a bit about where I have come to be: living the life of a Lightworker and Wayshower. Quite simply, a Wayshower helps to show others the way. The way *to what?* Well to their authentic selves, helping others to move along their own souls' paths. We Wayshowers can do this through teaching, coaching, encouraging, listening, energy clearing/resetting, or otherwise supporting our clients. Most Wayshowers also aspire to lead by example. But it is not a weighty obligation nor a pious position. It is a privilege and an honor, and So. Much. Fun!

A Wayshower is a form of Lightworker. A Lightworker is simply someone who brings Light (figuratively) into the world and helps to dispel darkness (also figuratively/spiritually). In my humble opinion, most newborn babies are Lightworkers by nature, as are our beloved pets. They bring us joy just by them being in our presence.

So, by now you might be thinking, "gee, this Linda person is really full of herself." Well no, that's not it at all. (Did I tell you yet that ANYONE can do what I do??) So now that I have explained a bit about the end (or current point) of my journey, let me take you back to the beginning, and perhaps you will choose to ride along.


## My path from Logical to Illogical... *or is it the other way around?*

*"If you don't know where you are going, any road will get you there"* – Lewis Carroll

I was born into a large, loving family. The concept of being "successful" was valued. For we children, "success" meant doing our chores, being respectful to others, and doing well in school. My parents modeled the behaviors of kindness and compassion, which were naturally woven through all facets of our life, but the tangible focus was good grades, a clean room, table manners, etc. These things were all logical, to some extent measurable, and quite easy to define. After all, Dad was an engineer by training and trade. And while Mom was a full-time mother and homemaker throughout my childhood, she was highly intelligent and creative. She read *Psychology Today* during her leisure time, applying her learnings to child-rearing and running a harmonious home.

When it was time for me to enroll in college, I first toyed with the education field. But what really held my interest was math and problem solving. In 1979, that meant one thing — Computer Science! It was a natural fit for me and the logical choice. I completed my bachelor's degree and went right into a career with one of the top local employers, where I stayed for most of the next 35 years, working my way up through the Information Technology department.

For the first 18 or so years, it was great! Life had been so easy. It was as if my path had chosen me, and I just needed to stay between the lines. But at some point, I started feeling a shift within me. I was restless and began feeling out of place in my corporate life. While I still found the work to be an interesting intellectual challenge, it just was not enough. The part of my job I enjoyed most was the part that had nothing to do with my job description—helping people with stress, issues, and seeking new paths. Apparently, I was unwittingly seeking MY new path! It was as if my logic-o-meter was ramping down while my inner self was starting to awaken.

Does this sound familiar to you and your path? If you are feeling a shift, do not ignore it. It could very well be Spirit offering you an opportunity of a lifetime!

What makes sense to my head vs. what makes sense to my soul

*"The journey of a thousand miles begins with a single step"* – Lao Tzu

In 1998, I came to understand the connection between my energy and my physicality in a very real way. I had chronic hip pain that I could not seem to shake. I contacted my neurosurgeon thinking that I might be having a recurrence of an earlier spinal issue. He instead referred me to a physiatrist, who did some basic tests and found nothing physically wrong with me, but he began to counsel me on job stress. I really did not put much stock in it at the time — yes, my job was high pressure, but I could handle it, right? I did not see how job stress would influence my hip pain being about an "8" on a 10-point scale, every day, for a year or so. That made no sense to me. It was illogical. So after several appointments with the nice doctor, I stopped seeing him. One of the gifts from the physiatrist however, was that he told me about Dr. Deepak Chopra. I listened to his audiobook "*The Seven Spiritual Laws of Success*", not just once but dozens of times, and I believe it really helped me to begin my awakening. What had been illogical before now became what made sense to me in a powerful way. Not in a way that I could explain with words, but in a way that felt "right" at my very core, my soul.

Let me pause here to offer an interesting footnote. The definition of a physiatrist is *"A physician who specializes in physical medicine and rehabilitation. Physiatrists specialize in restoring optimal function to people with injuries to the muscles, bones, tissues, or nervous system"*. There is NOTHING in this definition that would lead one to expect him to find a non-physical source of my physical pain. Until recently, I just assumed "physiatry" was a cross between "physiology" and "psychiatry". I now believe that I was sent to THAT particular physiatrist by my Guides to help me to begin my awakening.

*Ok, back to my story now.*

Several months after parting company with my physiatrist, I decided to leave my corporate job and strike out on my own in the consulting world. Wouldn't you know it—on my last day of work, I awoke with a noticeable lack of pain in my hip—the first time in well over a year it was at "0"! The good doctor was right! I sent him a letter to thank him for getting me going in the right direction. *Can physical pain have a non-physical source?* You bet it can!! In the years that followed, and even to this very day, my hip pain is typically non-existent. But whenever the pain creeps up to a "2" or more, I can always pinpoint what is stressing me out, address it, and voila, the pain goes away!

Fast forward about 12 years. Professionally, I was still living my corporate life but starting to actively seek a change. One of my sisters had started studying and practicing Reiki. She told me about it and thought that I might enjoy it too. And so my metaphysical studies began! As I became certified at the first two levels of Usui Reiki and began practicing, it was a bit surreal. I felt like I was "home" but at the same time, it was so foreign to me. I was not used to being a novice. It was both exciting and scary. *What if this wasn't real? What if the validation I received from my clients was fake? What if I failed?* But I continued on with my studies, flying on faith that this was where I was meant to be. My sister and I took Integrated Energy Therapy® (IET) training together–all levels right up through Master-Instructor. This all occurred over the course of about six months! Whoa!! I began teaching at a local metaphysical shop on weekends and working on friends in my home, while I continued my high-tech corporate job during the work week.

I still recall coming out of the metaphysical closet to my friends at work. This was a 180° shift for me! What would people think? At first, it was only to a few very close friends that I could reveal my newfound calling. But you know what—they did not call me crazy, and in fact, some asked me to work on them! Yes!! It was all falling into place and all making sense.

In 2014 I made the permanent switch. I left my corporate job and transitioned full-time to my vocation… my calling… my joy. The life of a Lightworker and Wayshower!

Everyday Magic is real

*"Magic is just something that you do not think is possible, until it happens for the first time!"* – Linda Huitt (yes, me, talking with some of my grandchildren about the reality of magic)

Have you ever experienced everyday magic? *Real* magic?? If your answer is "no", I challenge you to think again. This is the type of experience that you might think of as a miracle, or Divine intervention, or even a simple moment of synchronicity. Events or circumstances that you just cannot explain or justify, but with a positive and supportive outcome. It might be unnoticed at the time but becomes highly relevant later, in retrospect. Or perhaps it is noticed and feels "odd" but "right" in the moment, tapping into your sense of claircognizance (your inner "knowing").

You might wonder why I am talking about magic and what that has to do with the other side of the veil. I am offering this perspective so that you might open up in a new way to the metaphysical and Divine energy that is at play all around us, conspiring to support each of us on our soul's path. Getting more comfortable with this concept will help you to get a few steps closer to finding your own experiences beyond the veil.

One simple example of everyday magic is "time bending". Sometimes I will have a client who has booked a one-hour session, but once we talk, I realize the person is really in need of a more full, deep healing — a thorough session that typically requires 90 minutes to two hours. In those cases, I ask the Angels to make time to fit it all in… to bend the time… and they never disappoint. In fact, there is often extra time at the end to have a helpful conversation. It is magical! An important point on time bending — once you have made the request to your Angels or other higher power, it is best to pay little-to-no attention to the clock. Just trust that it will work out.

In another experience of everyday magic, I genuinely believe that my Angels and Guides conspired to save my life. I was working for a consulting firm in 2001, traveling each week to different major US cities to support various clients. I would fly out every Monday morning and return home every Friday night. I really loved the job. I got to do interesting work with smart and interesting colleagues, visit lots of fun cities, and spend every weekend at my home in Maine. What a dream! But that dream was cut short when the firm had to go through layoffs in the wake of the "Year 2000" flurry of anticipated corporate gloom-and-doom that (fortunately) did not manifest. I remember when I was told that I had been affected by the layoffs, I was not in the least bit upset. It felt right. I even said to my employers (who were extremely kind and compassionate), *"I'm fine–this just means that I'm supposed to be somewhere else now."* I have no idea how that calm notion made it into my head, other than perhaps the echoes of Dr. Chopra talking about dharma.

And I *was* fine. I landed another job back in Maine within about a month. Later that year, Mom broke her arm, and I thought that must have been the reason for my layoff—so that I could be closer to her and help with a few things—and I was very content with that being the reason.

But then, on September 11 of that year, we experienced the terrorist attack on the World Trade Center. In that attack, two of my colleagues perished. Two others made it out of the building, and two more were on their way in to the office when the attack occurred. One of these last two was a woman with whom I was co-assigned 98% of the time during my tenure with the firm, and the client was one that I had frequently served. In all likelihood, had I not been laid off, I would have been there during the attack. One of the two who perished, I later learned, had chosen to stay behind with a pregnant woman—something that would have been very characteristic of me had I been there. The aftermath of this event made it profoundly clear that my job on Earth was not yet complete. Often times what appears to be adversity in the moment can turn out to be just what you need to Divinely (and sometimes pretty assertively) guide you in the direction that best serves you and those around you. (Thank you, Angels!)

## My experiences beyond the veil

*"We are not human beings having a spiritual experience; we are spiritual beings having a human experience."* – Pierre Teilhard de Chardin

Let's get to the good stuff now: what I have personally experienced beyond the veil. What I love about visiting with the other side is that, for me, I am completely aware and conscious of what I am doing and able to remember and share the experiences.

I clearly remember my first experience journeying through the veil of the Angelic realm to meet with my Soul Counsel. In this journey (similar to the concept of a Shamanic journey), I was completely awake and aware of my physical surroundings. I literally felt the veil part, and gently wipe over my head and arms as I passed through. I then felt myself move through space and time, and then was able to feel the presence of the members of my Soul Counsel. We each have a Soul Counsel that collaborates with us to plan each of our lifetimes, to give us the rich experiences to further our soul's learning and ascension. In this first meeting, I was able to ask my Soul Counsel questions and "hear" their responses. I was in awe of how real this experience was, and it continues to be a new and beautiful experience each time I take my students through the veil.

Sometimes the other side of the veil comes to us, as I experienced in a workshop called "Quantum Spoon Bending" led by Gene Ang. Gene led us through a process that, in essence, changed the state of a common fork (because forks are more interesting than spoons to bend) to be malleable and easy to bend, and then harden again, without applying anything other than our own energy and intentions (i.e., no heat source was involved). How can that be? The easiest way I can reconcile it to my thinking brain is that we transported the molecules of the fork, temporarily, to a place and time where they were malleable. Long story short, in this workshop, I learned the importance of the word "allow" when it comes to all things metaphysical. At first, I had difficulty bending the fork due to negative self-talk, but once I got out of my thinking brain and began to "allow" the everyday magic to occur, bending the forks was easy.

Other times, the lines of the veil become blurred. For me, this happens in dreams. This is one of my favorite experiences because it is when I can visit with Mom, who left her physical body behind and returned to Spirit in 2010. She occasionally visits me in my dreams, and I see her vividly, in a state of wellness. We talk, hug, and laugh. And while my visits with Mom beyond the veil transcend space and time, for now they just exist when I am in a dream state of consciousness; we each return to our own side of the veil before I awake.

## Guiding others through the Veil

*"You have to grow from the inside out. None can teach you, none can make you spiritual. There is no other teacher but your own soul"* — Swami Vivekananda

I am so blessed that my Lightworker calling enables me to help others experience the wisdom and healing from the other side of the veil. My mission is to support others in returning to their natural state of joy and empowerment. In my healing practice, I conduct energy healing using Integrated Energy Therapy® (IET), Reiki, Melchizedek Method, and ThetaHealing®. I also provide empathic readings by accessing my clients' Akashic Records. I learned all of these techniques through formal training, and initially I practiced each modality discreetly and independently. Over time, I became comfortable with the fact that the energies blend and work very well together. I now incorporate several modalities into a single client session depending on each client's situation or need. And the more I practice, the more interesting the client experiences are that find their way to me. So many sessions begin with my client saying something like "you're going to think I'm crazy, but…", or "I don't expect you to believe me, but…". My clients are not crazy. They just have interesting and atypical experiences, and I love working with them. My intuition has become strong—a far cry from where I was less than ten years ago!

One of the clearest early examples of knowing that the wisdom being offered my client was not from "me", but from the other side of the veil, was during an Akashic Record Reading. My client was a woman with many questions for her Guides; I will call her Jane. One question was about her connection to Joe. I had no idea who Joe was to her—whether he was a friend, lover, family member, etc. But I just asked Jane's guides about how she and Joe were here to serve and support each other. I do not recall the details of the answer to that question (after all, the answers were for Jane, not for me), but I remember telling Jane, *"I don't know why, but they are showing me one of those red and white striped mints, like you get when you are leaving a restaurant."* That seemed pretty random to me, and not at all connected to Jane's question, but I have learned to share whatever messages I perceive. Jane's eyes opened wider, and later she told me, *"Joe is someone I recently started dating, and on our first date when we were leaving the restaurant, he filled my pocket with the red and white mints at the hostess stand."* Wow! Clearly, Spirit was telling Jane, in that moment, that the words I was sharing during the reading were not from me, but were from Jane's Guides.

More recently, one of my regular clients, who I will call Mary, told me that a home she had just moved into with her toddler daughter (who I will call Anna) seemed to have some spirits in it that were making them uncomfortable. As spirits do, they were messing with electronics. Mary sent me some photos of different parts of the home that were a bit eerie. Also, some of the things Anna was saying led Mary to believe the spirits were making themselves known to Anna, which was understandably a big concern to Mary. So Mary asked me to do a space clearing of the home, as well as some clearing on Anna. I did both, and also felt called to place an Angelic Heartbeam (an IET technique) in the home, near a window where the photos had shown the spirit silhouette.

Mary also called in a friend (who I will call Tim) with expertise in helping spirits to move along… yes, a real-life ghost buster! During

Mary's session with Tim, Mary became able to communicate with the spirits — a husband and wife with children, whose souls were continuing to reside in the home. Tim worked very compassionately to help the spirits to complete their transition to Heaven. As he did, the spirit wife described to Mary a column of light near the window that the children were extremely excited about it—yes, it was the Angelic Heartbeam! Tim continued to work with Mary and the spirit family, ultimately helping the family to board a horse-drawn coach, and travel to Heaven via the Heartbeam. A really beautiful experience all around!

Often at the start of a client session now, even before we begin the formal healing session or reading, as my client explains why they came to see me, I settle into channeling. As my client talks, I open myself to connect to my higher powers, ALWAYS with a bubble of protection around us first. I close my eyes, and words just start to come. It might sound like it is coming from me, but I know that it is not. I start to "know" things that I do not know. Inspired perspectives come to me to share, that I have no personal basis to offer. Often this becomes a spontaneous guided meditation for my client, and our Guides take us on a journey full of symbolism, offering lovely empowering and supportive visions during that journey.

## I am home

*"Be grateful for the home you have, knowing that at this moment, all you have is all you need."* — Sarah Ban Breathnach

It has been one step at a time for me along this journey, with each step pulling me deeper into my Spiritual awareness, with peaceful comfort, and connecting me with the other side the veil. I was recruited by my Higher Power, and I am so happy that I answered the call. I never know what opportunities my Guides will bring to me. After all, that's part of being a warrior. And yes, I am ready, as always, for my next assignment!

## About the Author

### LINDA ANZELC HUITT

Linda's mission is to assist her clients in finding greater joy in life, while restoring their personal empowerment and accountability. She does this with private energy sessions for people and pets, as well as public and private training events, through her metaphysical healing practice, Pathway Of Joy. She also offers empowerment coaching to help her clients move past perceived personal, interpersonal, energetic, and technical challenges.

A unique combination of life experiences gives Linda perspective to relate to a broad spectrum of clients. She grew up in a large, loving, and hard-working family in rural Maine. After earning a bachelor's degree in Computer Science, the first 30 years of her adult life were spent in a high-tech corporate management career. In 2012, being drawn to a more spiritual path, she began actively studying and practicing holistic and metaphysical techniques, and transitioned full-time to her healing and coaching vocation in 2014.

The Pathway Of Joy studio is located in Buxton Maine. Linda also serves clients and students from across the US, Canada, and Central America, through phone and video connections. She resides in Buxton with her husband Mike and their feline babies. Linda and Mike love camping, road trips, paddling, quiet time at home together, and spending time with their children and grandchildren.

Email: PathwayOfJoy1111@gmail.com

Website: www.PathwayOfJoy.com
Facebook: @PathwayOfJoy
Instagram: @Pathway_Of_Joy
YouTube: Pathway Of Joy
Clubhouse: @LindaHuitt
Alignable: Pathway Of Joy
Nextdoor: Pathway Of Joy

# THREE

## Sandra Joy

### YOUR SIXTH SENSE WILL GUIDE YOU

"Hey Sandi!" My eyes flew open, and I jolted up in my bed. Why the hell is my sister yelling at me at 3:30 in the morning? She's really going to get it for waking me up. I became conscious of being in my bedroom, my husband sleeping peacefully next to me, and my heart pounding. I KNEW my sister was there despite the fact that she lived on the other side of the state. I heard her. I convinced myself it was just a dream and went back to sleep. Daily life took over, and I forgot all about it. A few days later, a welfare check was called in because no one had heard from her, and I received a call that my sister had been found deceased. She passed away in her sleep a few days earlier. I realized that she really WAS in my room that night, and she had wanted my attention to tell me she had passed away. We always had long talks about the spiritual side of life, intuition, and connecting to our "superpowers", as we liked to call them. She knew I'd get her message.

We are born with six senses, but most people end up with five because they unknowingly shut one down. It is our intuition that slowly fades away through societal upbringing. There are many reasons why intuition is lost in the fray of life. When I was a child growing up in my family home, I remember knowing things that I had no way of explaining. I knew who was calling before the phone was answered (back before the days of caller ID and cell phones), I could "read" the energy of a room just by walking into it. I instinctively knew my mother's emotions without her expressing them. I even knew when to come home when I was out playing with my neighborhood friends. These were gut feelings that I could not explain; I just knew.

## TRUSTING YOUR GUT AND LISTENING TO YOUR INNER VOICE

My mother told me that sometimes she would think about having me come home at a certain time, which wasn't our agreed-upon time, and all she would have to do was think about it, and I would show up. I would get these gut feelings that I just had to go home. We joked and called it our ESP (extra sensory perception).

We thought it was just a silly joke, but it was actually what was happening in reality. I was picking up thoughts from my mom as she put them out into the universe, willing me to come home. I listened to my gut instinct which told me to go home early. I didn't have a reason to go home early, it was just a feeling that I had. When I was little, I followed those feelings; and they didn't just come through my mother. My father also had his moments of unexplainable clarity.

One summer before I started seventh grade, I was sitting at the dinner table with my mom, dad, sister, niece, and nephew. My nephew wanted to go ride bikes after dinner. There was no reason in the world for us not to be permitted to go. However, my father adamantly refused to let us. I was stubborn at 12 years old and did not take no for an answer. I asked my mom why we couldn't go. I wanted a good reason other than the standard "Because I said so" answer, but my father couldn't give a reason; he just said he didn't have a good feeling about it. I didn't stop asking, and eventually, my father gave in to our request. About 20 minutes after we left, a neighbor came running down the street to my parents' house to get them because I had crashed. Not just a simple skinned knees kind of crash. I had flipped over the handlebars and tore out a chunk of my leg. It was definitely an emergency room trip; stitches and no walking for a while. My dad knew something bad was going to happen, but he couldn't quite put his finger on it. He finally caved and allowed me to go out; however, he should've trusted his intuition and kept me home. He would've had a cranky girl for a while, but things would've been a lot better than they ended up being. Now, I have a pretty good size scar on my leg, reminding me of the fact that intuition exists and we should trust it.

Have you ever heard those stories about the people who didn't get on the airplane, and the airplane crashed, and everyone on board perished? They didn't have a reason for not getting on the plane, except they knew something bad was going to happen, and they just listened to their intuition. They trusted themselves and survived. It is not always easy to trust ourselves when we are taught not to trust our instincts and our intuition from a very young age. Oftentimes we ignore our intuition and end up in precarious circumstances as a result—like being in a relationship, accepting or leaving a job, or even walking out of the house that day. There are many different examples of how intuition can help guide you in the right direction. Many of the struggles that we deal with on a day-to-day basis can be alleviated if we would just learn to tune in to ourselves instead of powering through like society expects us to do.

You can learn to tune in to your intuition in many ways. Sometimes the feeling is so overwhelming that there is no ignoring it. Unfortunately, we live in a society where we are told to push those feelings down and do what we're told to do. However, it doesn't have to be this way.

## DECODING YOUR BODY'S PHYSICAL FEELINGS

Listening to your inner voice, your intuition, can become easier for you with some practice. The first thing to do is to tune in to the way your body feels in certain situations. We get physical signals that let us know our intuition is working, and it's like a clue to tune in to our feelings. Similar to walking into a room and immediately noticing the energy in the space is negative. You might feel as if there had just been an argument or that you just walked in and interrupted someone's conversation even though no one said anything. Those are physical signals that you get in your body that tell you that something is off.

Keeping track of your feelings in a notebook you carry, a note app on your phone, or even writing a journal entry at the end of your day can really help you discover patterns. When you discover these patterns, you can see the results of your intuition and whether or not you were spot on or if it was off a little. Everything is energy, and everything has a vibration. Feelings have a vibration too. Consider why you can comfortably welcome someone into your personal space or feel very uncomfortable if someone is unwelcome in your space. You may not know why; it's just an immediate feeling you have. It is the energetic vibration; the energy the other person is giving off, which your energy mingled with and you picked up on. What you are experiencing is your sixth sense: your intuition. There can be many different signals your body can give you. You may get a gut feeling where your stomach feels like it's on a roller coaster, you may get a slight or intense headache, you may even feel ill to the point where you need to sit down or remove yourself from a situation completely. When you keep track of all of these signals every time they happen, also keep track of what your responses were. Did you listen to your intuition and respond accordingly, or did you ignore your intuition and experience negative results? Keep track of everything you experience and the results of your choices.

Writing your experience down may seem taxing at first, but you will quickly develop a routine. Having notes that you can look back on can bring you considerable clarity as well as show you how much you have grown your intuition. Practicing purposeful self-reflection through journaling does wonders for your confidence and helps to silence the doubting and negative self-talk that may show up every now and then.

## BUILDING CONFIDENCE BY TRYING OUT WHAT WORKS FOR YOU

Trusting yourself is the biggest hurdle you have to get over. You're going to convince yourself you're crazy, you're making it up, and you couldn't possibly know these things because you've been taught to back up what you say with examples, and here you are without a single one. When it comes to intuition, you don't have the examples to back it up until after the fact. Sometimes the validation that your intuition was correct comes days, weeks, or even months after your intuitive nudge. Trust the process, and most importantly, trust yourself. There's a difference between learning to trust your intuition by noticing synchronicities and grasping at straws when a sign doesn't show up for you. Microscopic analysis does not work in situations like these. You either know it, or you don't. The answers or feelings will be there, or they won't. Pushing yourself to try to form connections and synchronicities that don't exist just sets you farther behind on truly connecting to and learning how to use your intuition.

Sometimes you even get stuck in a pattern of disbelieving yourself or being around people who also need proof that can't be provided, so you modify your behavior to fit. There was a time when my family and I were driving about an hour and a half away to pick up our son's new car. There was a lot of traffic, and one of the major interstates was closed. There was no reason for it to be closed, we couldn't see anything wrong. There were no news reports out yet that said what was happening. Then, our son pipes up from the backseat and says, "I think it was a police chase." Now, in the area where we live, police chases are fairly uncommon. Immediately, my husband and I laughed and shut him down, saying there's no way it can be a police chase, because they don't happen around here. Then my husband went into "explanation mode" on reasons why it could not possibly be a police chase. Here we are, parents of an intelligent, responsible young man, looking for physical proof to back up his claim that it was a police chase. He had no physical proof, just his gut instinct. It turned out that it WAS a police chase. We were rerouted onto several back roads because the chase ended badly in a crash. It was one of those moments of disbelief that the universe throws into your path every now and then to wake you up and say, "hey, get back in tune with yourself!" Our son was in tune with himself, and he said what he felt, and he was 100% correct.

I have learned through working with my clients, and even people who just stop by my crystal shop, that there are energies I connect with and energies I do not connect with. I know whether someone is open and available to talk about spirituality and crystal energetics and how they work, and I know when people are closed off and unwilling to take part in a conversation about what I do. Sometimes, the feelings are so strong it overtakes me, and I end up telling someone very personal things about them that I get through what I call downloads. I did not always listen to these downloads or trust them; this was a system of trial and error. Although, I should call it a system of apprehension and trust instead. I had no idea where I was getting this information; it would just come to me as a feeling or a thought. I thought I was making it up, and it was all in my head. Well, it was in my head, but I wasn't making it up. The rational part of my mind took over and said, "Ok, maybe things are just very general, and I am really being so non-specific that they are able to make a connection to anything and say that it's correct. So, I started really tuning into my intuition and my downloads, and I started being extremely specific. I noticed that when I would talk to people about things, I would get a *feeling* as well as *knowing*. I would express the *feelings* as emotions, and I would say, "I'm feeling very angry right now..." "I'm feeling very frustrated right now..." or "I'm feeling really happy right now..." Sometimes I would just break out into laughter, having no rational idea why this was happening. I trusted myself and said what was on my mind. It was like ideas were just popping into my head that weren't mine. I just followed my instincts and shared the thoughts I had. 100% of the time, they were correct. My confidence was increasing.

I remember the first time I talked to a stranger about this connection and the messages I had for him. It didn't start off so well. I found you have to ease people into it if they don't know you or know what you're about. I started by saying, "I receive downloads from spirit, and if you're open to receiving them, I would like to share messages I've gotten for you." Usually, people are thrilled and say yes. Sometimes they say no and move along. I never take offense. The first time I ever did this for someone I didn't know was for a man browsing in my crystal shop. I started off asking for permission, and when given permission to continue, I immediately went into discrediting the person's entire line of work. It was a very awkward situation. I felt the person get defensive and start closing down, and I thought, OK, there's more to this I need to go through first, so let me see where this is going.

Luckily, he was a patient enough person and let me really think through where all of this was coming from. Once I sorted through the information I got, it turned out to be the most powerful intuition reading I had done to that point. Had I allowed myself to get caught up in the flustered frustration at the beginning, he would have never received the information he needed to hear. In fact, as soon as I leaned into my trust, I received more downloads than I could keep up with. I trusted myself so much that when he was reaching for a connection and tried to make the puzzle fit, I would correct him and say no, that's not it. It was a feeling I got in my gut knowing I was 100% right about it, and I followed my instinct without any shred of proof whatsoever. I told this gentleman what line of work he was in, why he was in it, and what his purpose was moving forward in his line of work. The information was extremely specific, and by the time I was done, he was in tears because he had so many questions going through his mind about his job and whether he should continue in it or not. He never shared that with me. I just got this overwhelming feeling to share this download with him. The message was exactly what he needed when he needed it. In fact, the total massacre of his profession at the beginning that had really flustered me turned out to be a reflection of *his* doubt about *his* chosen profession. Yes, *his* emotion was coming out with the words *I* spoke. I'm a genuinely considerate person, and I was a bit shocked when I heard myself speaking to him. If I would not have trusted my intuition to connect with him and share this information, he would not have received the Divine messages he was meant to get that day.

You don't have to use your intuition to connect to others to pass along information from the Divine, you can learn to tune in to your intuition simply to benefit yourself and help you along your path.

## DEVELOPING YOUR CLAIR(S)

There are several types of ways intuition operates. They are: clairvoyance (seeing), clairaudience (hearing), claircognizance (knowing), clairsentience (feeling), clairalience (smelling), and clargustance (tasting). These are commonly referred to as clairs. There are many different ways you can develop your clairs to learn how to receive information. Everybody is born with full access to their intuition through one or more of the clairs. I know what you're thinking— how do you know which one(s) is yours? A good way to start practicing connecting to your intuition and discovering your clair(s) is to use the five senses you already trust.

What are you seeing? What comes into your field of vision that could be a sign for you? Is it something that just crossed your path and it brings back an old memory? Why is that memory significant? Connect the dots. Just like the childhood game we used to play when we traced one circle to the next to ultimately create an image we could recognize. Your senses can give you the dots to connect. Listen to what you hear (clairaudience). Is there a word or a phrase that stands out in someone's conversation as they pass you by? Is there a song on the radio that's meaningful to you? Do you hear words spoken when no one is around? What about the scent of flowers or certain food cooking (clairalience). What memories stir up for you? Even the taste of food or drink can be a signal to something you need to tune in to (clargustance). Maybe you get pictures in your mind that you can see clearly (clairvoyance), or just know something that you didn't know moments earlier (clairsentience). These are all ways to consciously tune in to your intuition and notice the way(s) it works best.

You don't need to be hyper-aware every second of every day. To do so would be very overwhelming. Your body's physical reaction will tell you when it's meaningful to you. You'll have the feeling you *just have to* look something up, or you *just have to* talk to a person, or you *just have to* be in a certain place at a certain time. The more you practice, the better you will get when recognizing the moments your intuition is tapping you on the shoulder. Don't beat yourself up if you know you've missed a signal or a sign or you chose not to follow your intuition. Remember when my sister came to visit me in the middle of the night, and then life just took over? I didn't beat myself up for not calling her. We find things out when we're meant to find things out. Everything happens at the time it's supposed to happen; but, it doesn't have to be as difficult as we make it. You still have free will, and you can make your own choices. You can choose to live in low vibrational energy that attracts all things negative like stress, anxiety, frustration, anger, disease, etc.—or you can choose to live in high vibrational energy, which attracts all things positive like abundance, health, joy, happiness, etc.…

Think about it, in order to survive through infancy we have to use our intuition. We know when we're hungry, we know when we're tired, we know when we need affection, we know when we want to go to someone new or if we want to stay with someone familiar. Not surprisingly, it is exactly at this age that society starts conditioning us to ignore our intuition. Some parents allow their children to go to a friend to be held and cuddled, but the child is very uncomfortable and wants nothing to do with that particular friend. The parent sees no reason why the child is acting out and encourages them to interact. The trusted parent inadvertently teaches the child to ignore their intuition and do what they're told, thus beginning the pattern of intuition numbing behavior. Children have this uncanny ability to express themselves and exactly what they're thinking and feeling.

They *just know* when to ask for what they need. It is this intuition that you are connecting back into now.

You've always had it, you've just buried it through societal conditioning. You've learned to power through, you've learned to ignore your gut and to silence it yourself. You become numb to your intuition by overriding it with certain behaviors like people pleasing, conforming to social groups, and even your job performance expectations. When in fact, connecting to your intuition would actually help you decrease the stress and anxiety that doing those things brings. All you have to do is trust yourself.

## SIGNS AND SIGNALS FROM THE UNIVERSE: IS THIS MIC ON? (*tap* *tap*)

There are signs and signals all around us that show us we're on the right track. Have you ever experienced déjà vu? Déjà vu could be one of the ways the universe is trying to tell you that you're on the right path. How about when something happens, and you were just thinking about it? For example, seeing the exact make of a car you were just talking about or running into a person who unexpectedly popped into your head. These are called synchronicities. It is one way we can check in with the universe to make sure our intuition is working properly. We can also receive messages through numbers and number patterns. Especially double, triple, and quadruple digits. Even number sequences that are not repetitive but are meaningful to us in some way, like an old house address or a certain date, can hold information for us. Keep track of when you see these synchronicities and ask yourself how they apply to your current situation. You may pass these signs off as coincidence when they are really messages meant to guide you.

When I talk to clients, one of the commonalities I recognize is a victimhood perspective. People generally ask, "Why is everything bad happening to me?" There are a lot of places to go with that question, but the first place I start is by asking my client what kind of energy they are putting out into the world? If you're constantly giving off negative energy because you're focusing on negative things, then you are apt to miss these incredible intuitive signs from the universe that are there to guide you. Normally, people in this mindset don't connect to their intuition, and they're missing the roadmap, which, in turn, makes them complain about how hard life is or how unfair things are when they had the answers inside of them all along. They just needed to tune in and listen.

Another way I have found to connect with messages from the universe, and my intuition is through nature in the form of animals. Sometimes, I'll see an animal unexpectedly, and instead of just saying, "Oh, there's a beautiful fox," I will look up the meaning of a fox because there is something that is connected to my life at the moment that is connected to the sighting of the fox. Everything has a meaning, everything is connected, and if you are open and aware, you will receive these messages and will connect deeply to your intuition. You've probably had that feeling of regret when you should have listened to your gut, but you chose to ignore it instead. I definitely have.

You are reading this today because I chose to stop ignoring my intuition: I was meant for something bigger. Actually, I tried to ignore that message for a very long time. The longer I ignored my intuition, the worse my life became. I was so stubborn, fearful, and programmed that I fought against what I knew was the right move for me. I fought so hard that I had to be brought to my senses through a terrible experience; an accident that left me physically broken and bleeding, before I started paying attention to my intuition. Now, almost eight years later, I have fully embraced the path that I knew I needed to follow. I love what I do for others now. Watching someone connect to their true purpose and seeing their light shining brightly is pretty fulfilling. I love helping to guide people out of their pain and into their purpose. The first step is reconnecting to yourself. Tune in, learn to trust yourself and the messages you are receiving from spirit. Learn to identify the signs of intuition that are your guiding light. Intuition is your most powerful asset, and you can learn to reconnect.

If you would like more information about working with me to unlock your "superpowers," visit my website, SandraJoy.com, and send me a message. You can also join my free group, Untame Your Soul and Unleash Unlimited Abundance, on Facebook. There are several ways to work with me, and I would be honored to walk with you.

## About the Author

### SANDRA JOY

Sandra Joy is the founder and CEO of Healing Realms, LLC and Sandra Joy, LLC. She embraces the new energy consciousness of Earth and guides others to embrace this energy to connect and thrive in their soul purpose.

She is an Adult Indigo with a deep connection to Indigo, Crystal, and Diamond Children as well as a highly intuitive clairsentient. She is a Lightworker certified with Hands of Light, a Master Usui Reiki Practitioner, a Crystal and Color Energies Expert, a certified Hypnotherapist, certified Oracle Card reader, and a 20 year activator of Indigo and Crystal Children.

Her purpose in this lifetime is to connect with people who want to learn how to harness the power of their energy system and thrive in their soul's purpose. She lives in Pennsylvania on a small farm with her husband, son, daughter, and many animals.

Email: HealingRealms111@gmail.com
Website: SandraJoy.com
Facebook:
https://www.facebook.com/groups/UnTameYourSoul
https://www.facebook.com/untameyoursoul
Instagram: @the.sandra.joy
TikTok: @SandraJoySol
Clubhouse: @SandraJoySol

# FOUR

## Carole Griffiths

### THE PSYCHIC BLOODLINE

### How It All Began

Growing up as a child in the 1960s with a parent who can only be described as a super psychic was quite an experience. My father possessed amazing gifts, and with his quirky and fun character, life never ran along normal channels. Intermittently there would be bursts of crazy energy with my dad responding to something unseen and unheard, which was both absorbing and alarming at the same time. He would hold full conversations with those we would call 'ghosts' often when in 'sensitive company'. Nevertheless, it was the norm in our household, and his behaviours were accepted by varying degrees by those who witnessed it.

My grandmother, his mother, also carried the same psychic gifts. She lived a four-hour drive from us in south England and with us living in north England, it meant we were only able to visit her around twice a year. She, in turn, would come and stay with us too, but still, we did not have much time to spend with her. During those occasions, she would get her Tarot cards out and provide us all with readings giving away advice along with your childish secrets to everyone whether you liked it or not. She did not possess a filter! Although this experience was usually an excruciating one for me, I also found it most fascinating, particularly as I knew that those same energies ran through my veins also. She loved her cards, but her favourite of all was reading tea leaves. On one occasion, while reading her leaves, she announced to my mother that she would have four children. My mum, then age 37 and already having three children from age nine years and upwards, laughed this off but did indeed give birth again within the next 11 months, completing her set of four children as predicted by my granny. She was a real force to be reckoned with and is so dear to my heart. I was also so very blessed with the most wonderful parents.

Only in recent times, I have been furnished with the information that my paternal grandfather was also in possession of the psychic gift. I had no idea of this at all; for me it was amazing news. He lived in India and died there when I was four years old, and I never met him. It also explains why my dad had such a high concentration of his gift.

## The Lady

From age four upwards, I had a total awareness of another world aside from regular life. I used to whisper to nothing in particular asking. 'Where did I come from?' A great stillness would then follow. During those times, I used to be 'visited' by a woman whom I named 'The Lady'. I had heard of the existence of Guardian Angels, but I knew this presence was different. The Lady felt so special, and all her focus was on me and my well-being; she seemed to know me very well. How she communicated to me, though, with such love also included what I would DO later in life. She offered me such immense love and assurance that I would be ok, I felt the utmost security at those times. I would only ever have to have a suggestion of thought, and there she would be. She guided, coun-selled, and fed me spiritually.

Her visits regularly continued for the next few years; however, I became increasingly aware of my parent's reaction to my psychic ability. There seemed to be real concern because of my tendency to blurt out insight and predictions, and it soon became clear that that was totally unacceptable. I had no control over my gift whatsoever, and it was difficult for me to sort out what was 'real' in a regular sense and what was not. School was difficult for me, and I was often bored and accused of daydreaming. My teachers reported that I had a vivid imagination, but the reality was I was channelling information that made so much more sense to me. I hoped one day to make good use of what appeared to be different, which at the same time I knew was most important. Over time I learned to dumb down what I freely blurted out but can still have episodes of that now, surprising myself and others. It can be awkward then having to explain my outburst, but it is mostly nowadays accepted with great interest.

During those early years, the messages placed in the hands of a child were profound and felt to be of extreme importance. It felt like 'old advice', things I already knew but had forgotten. It was as though I was remembering something against learning something new. The feeling of authority from this Lady felt higher than even the authority of my parents, and I listened keenly. My comprehension of it was that it was a sole mission I was required to complete; to the child me, I was not daunted by it in any way. There was a real sense of security that I would find a way to do this.

Impressions I received during these times from life going on around me seemed to go against what I inwardly knew. I found it astounding that some of those older than me, who I was apparently meant to learn from, brought conditions totally against what I was taught by The Lady. Her perfect concept of love and care of others was often trashed by behaviours I saw around me. There were times I would feel disoriented, between two worlds but fully leaning only one way to the magical world that was in my blood. I really was on a sole/soul mission, and I fully intended to put my all into it.

That initial awareness continues still for me to this day; basically, it is who I Am. Whenever I receive transmissions of that nature, it is extremely intense; a feeling of energies gathering and re-arranging themselves, bringing the truth of that moment. All my senses heighten, which causes me to feel highly alert. It gets my attention! These occurrences can happen anywhere and without warning. There is no bugle call or announcement of any kind. It is just Boom! Spirit used to tell me that I have a valve that was left open when I was born. I now know that to be my third eye being open to a much higher awareness than human life can provide. I have learned how to handle it very well, and you could be standing right in front of me and not realise what is happening within me when you speak. During a transmission, I can have one message impressed on me in a flash, a split second. For me, then to go on and explain what just happened, though, could take up to an hour to produce it in normal human speak. It is as though a whole strong and intense conversation is 'impressed upon me' in just what we would view as 'one moment of time'.

The early incidents were pivotal occurrences that continue to shape my life, indeed all my moments since I live and breathe the depth of what I was taught in my formative years.

Through The Lady I was taught that we are all the same, that we all have the same potential to achieve anything we want. I would talk to her about what I did not think I had, but wanted, and her message was always the same, 'what do you have?' Hindsight has taught me the benefit of this message, but it took many years for me to really grasp that concept. What she was speaking of was the importance of gratitude and honouring everything in the present moment rather than quickly bypassing that for the next 'wanted thing'. What you have right now in this exact moment is all that you have to work with. See the blessing in the present moment.

She talked to me about the higher realms, of Heaven, the Angels and Guides on our individual path, of consciousness, about what every soul was trying to do and why. Her Truth still stands out so strongly for me. Her loving presence was a real blessing and treasure to me and continues so.

As I became older, my gifts became like a tapping on my shoulder, a reminder of what I knew I had to do. There was a sense of urgency but with no pressure whatsoever. At age 15 years, I freely gave readings to my classmates at school during lunch breaks, often getting into trouble and being reprimanded. I had a strong inkling that my gifts were not for frivolous purposes and pulled back from that. Briefly, the Lady would visit, but, in all honesty, I held her away from me as life took over.

## The Psychic Journey Continued

During my 20's I worked as a secretary. This work had no meaning to me, and I began a new quest to re-engage with what I felt had been left behind. I searched out books on spirituality which were very few and far between in those days. I taught myself to meditate. I began to visit spiritualist churches and receive messages that did not come from 'myself'. This was a real breakthrough for me. There was a strong theme that always came through for me via psychic mediums who seemed to single me out from the crowd. Their message was, 'One day, you will be doing what I am doing'. I was very shy in those days and could not imagine that I could ever conduct myself that way; however, I became very hooked on anything remotely spiritual.

In my 30's as a young mother, I experienced a major turning point. I came across an advertisement for a newly opened local Spiritual Awareness Centre that ran development courses. The courses were residential, not to mention expensive, and I managed to strike a deal for 'this education' by volunteering to help in the kitchen and serving the students lunches in exchange for tuition. That was readily agreed upon. On embarking on this exciting new journey, I was thrust into accelerated development through a wonderful medium who later became a very dear friend. She pushed me hard, forcing me to overcome my shyness and give messages to her students. It did not occur to me until later that she considered me a teacher rather than a student. We undertook deep meditations every day and performed weekly physical demonstrations with dearly departed spirits coming to visit. Around the room, musical instruments, rain sticks, etc. were placed, anything they could 'use' to show their presence. We had 'regulars' who would come through every single time. We helped lost souls to accept their newfound position and lovingly helped them to fully cross over. We also performed healing that was so powerful that it would move you to tears.

Through spiritual advice I personally received around this time, I engaged in working on Healing my Inner Child, which was incredible. This process involves spending time with your own inner child, nurturing them, reassuring them that you are always there for them, just loving them. This became addictive, most important, and I continually spend much time doing this, it is so gratifying. Only you yourself know what you really need and are therefore the best person to provide this. The healing attained is incredible, and I encourage all to try this. Your inner child receives what is missing for them, and both versions of you are healed at once in one Holy moment.

Following these wonderful days with the Spiritual Awareness Centre, my spiritual growth took a huge upward turn. From then onwards, I pushed myself hard to carry out the work that I came here to do and, at last, fully followed my calling. I engaged in providing psychic services in person and then later online to great success with daily demand ever-increasing. Throughout the years, I have served tens of thousands of clients, and their gratitude during the moments of their readings resides within me and always will. The blessing is mine also.

Before we come into an earth body, with the help of our Guides and spiritual loved ones, we draw up a soul contract according to what we want to achieve in our next lifetime. When providing readings for my clients, I am initially told about their soul urges and receive knowledge on what their soul is trying to do. Every life has a theme which the soul has individually chosen to undertake. All are on a mission with great enthusiasm about the human journey with the sole intention of expanding their spiritual soul. This process is intricate, with many threads like a life tapestry. We choose every character in our lives, the heroes, and the villains, and all will play their part in order for us to achieve what we came here to do. Our heroes are our biggest supporters, and inwardly we just know them at deep levels; we feel safe with them. However, it is often difficult to view our own villains as of any benefit to our lives, but they are performing a role in our lives to assist us in achieving our important goal. They shape who we become. It is not important how long we will battle our villains for and deal with them but obviously, the sooner the better! Your worst enemy can be your best friend in the spirit world who is lovingly challenging you to transcend conditions that you should not be spending so much time on in order to get to the best bit! When we draw up our soul contract, at the time it all sounds so easy, not to mention fun, but the amnesia that also accompanies us on our entrance to the human existence is our greatest blessing. It prompts us to reach and search for who we really are, and then just be that. At our base, humans are pure love.

The guidance that spirit brings through my readings is always personal to the client. They are geared to your hot topic of the day, to your past, present, and future. To whatever you want to talk about. Your own Guide will meet with mine to bring pertinent messages that relate directly to what you are striving for. They dig deep into your life and times, tell you what others around you are doing, and often what you can adjust in your own corner to achieve what frustratingly seems to elude you. Messages are usually your wake-up call. Spirit can stop you in your tracks when you are on a path that is not the best for you. They can break behaviours that you have been engaged in for too long, given what you said you wanted to do. Some clients need only one or two readings, others want more frequent guidance. The guidance is often just a reminder to each soul of how they can help themselves regardless of what anyone else is doing around them. When you change, everything else will change and not before. Spirit put you back on your real path, facing forward and give you a loving shove. They will cover every single area of your life that you want to ask about, whether it be family, finances, career, love, health, etc. There is nothing that is off-limits. As life becomes more and more busy for us all, to drop everything and receive guidance can be pure bliss, to take your foot off the pedal and just do YOU.

My psychic work is like soul food for me. It has always been my true passion. The right client will draw to me at the right time through their own psychic ability, of which they believe they have none! Accessing psychic advice allows you to realise your true potential and assists you in moving towards your true-life purpose. To see the change in clients from when we first meet until they leave is a blessing in itself. I receive along with the client the very same blessings, and that is always the intention of those who guide us.

## Quantum Healing Hypnosis Technique (QHHT)

Along with being able to engage fully in this lifelong psychic passion each day, I am also blessed to be a trained Level 2, QHHT practitioner (Quantum Healing Hypnosis Technique), having trained under Dolores Cannon herself in the UK a few months before she passed away in 2014.

The process is remarkable and in-depth; It is all-consuming. It begins with a deep interview which brings about a complete overview of the client's life thus far, during which time their higher self is totally involved. This forms an 'agreement' to work at deeper levels during the actual hypnosis. Following on from this and during the induction period, the client enters a state of hypnosis at the Theta level of consciousness through which they can be guided to journey back to previous lifetimes which are relevant to the current one. The same life themes are immediately apparent even though the surrounding conditions are totally different. They are guided through each lifetime, sometimes up to four lifetimes, and after each, they can see the totality of what they really wanted to achieve and how well that was met. They can see where they took wrong turns, and they can see excesses of human behaviour that were detrimental to their initial cause. Most of all, they know what they could/should have done! Great eagerness is then present to 'try again in another lifetime'. There is no shame or blame of self, only more knowledge on how to expand their soul further. Following this stage, the client can then access their own higher self, who holds all knowledge of them. The client's questions can then be asked, and healing can be lovingly performed; healing can be accepted here with no resistance.

All clients leave with certainly much more than they arrived with; they leave with a full understanding of why they are here along with a mission they cannot wait to embark on, which is incredible. Having been the recipient of this fascinating process through other practitioners has been a true highlight for me. To find 'another you' in 'another form' yet with your own unique consciousness is amazing. Compassion for self is a natural result. Many can find it easy to have compassion for others yet can fail to nurture their own self. These 'other versions' of yourself are most acceptable to you since they ARE you!

Being psychic, I offer any messages received from spirit following a QHHT session which is always readily accepted. During the interview stage, I receive so many insights and messages for the client, I scribble them all down and deliver them later so as to not influence their session. Whilst they are 'under' I can often 'see' the client in their lifetime and receive the vividness of their experiences, along with how any situation makes them feel. Many clients report that I am also present in their lifetimes; it is always that 'this me' appears for them as a bystander, at the front of a crowd, etc. I do not know how that works, but I like to think that they feel safe knowing I am there to watch over them and guide them.

My first experience of exchanging a session with another practitioner was very daunting for both of us as we qualified around the same time and were as inexperienced as each other. The first session was a wonderful experience. We were both so in awe of what we each 'just did'! This now friend and fellow practitioner and I experienced such amazing results that we then felt prompted to train at a higher level still. Our Level 2 training took place in the magical town of Glastonbury, England, from where many legends spring. Other sessions followed on from the first, which also led to real and meaningful psychic exchanges and will always stand out in my memory.

## Message from Spirit

Earth experiences are intensely challenging in these times. There is so much coming at us all at once; the pace of life feels speeded up, and many souls can feel overwhelmed. With emails, social media, and instant communications racing at us all our waking moments, connecting to your own guidance becomes even more important and indeed should be a priority for all. The fastest way to re-connect to the source of your being is through meditation and mindfulness. Every soul has the ability to tap into the same source that lovingly feeds us in all our moments. On this topic, spirit has this message for you to activate your inner senses to assist you on your life path:

'Disconnect quickly and go within. Within you contains the totality of your wisdom and everything you need to know in any given moment of your life. There you will find your own unique space, which will bring you instant comfort. From that place springs a knowingness that all is well and as it should be. You can gain peace for as long as you stay there; you will be untouched by the pressure and stress that life places upon you. It is there that your inspirations for anything and everything resides. It is a space that enables you to receive what you need in any given moment. We eagerly await your presence and attention so that we may guide you in ways you do not have time to think of yourself. Your emotions are your true guidance system. You are here to experience them but not get caught up in them. Look to where you are placing your attention and turn away from what you know does not serve you. We thank you for your agreement to visit the earth during these times, you are strong souls who fully contribute to the whole. Never underestimate your contribution nor your importance. We are here, so please proceed'.

## The Lady Re-Appeared

You may wonder what happened to The Lady. She has always been in my consciousness, and any thought of her gives me a warm, heartfelt, and loving feeling; there is always the same feeling of safety. A few years ago, which was in actuality decades later, following our initial conversation, I experienced the mindset to meditate to try to access her once again. I felt rather embarrassed that I had not talked to her in so long but knew I would receive her ready forgiveness. I entered a state of meditation, and before I could finish my thought and request, she was there. I had an instant recognition; a sense of knowingness that was all consuming. In that moment, I immediately knew who The Lady was and, as a result, experienced one of the most moving experiences of my life. The Lady was me! THIS version of me. The one who provided the inner child healing at those earlier times and who continued to provide me with the same blessings. Across decades whenever I accessed the child me, 'she' received the love, care, understanding, and reassurance that 'this version of me' offered her. Only I knew what she felt and needed. It was all received. My soul rocked on its axis at that point. It all made perfect sense, the feeling of familiarity, the sense of knowing I could rely on this Lady with my total being. The fact that she 'already knew' I would be ok purely because she was ok in the 'here and now' was mind-blowing. To know there is a future version of you who knows everything about you is just incredible.

Please talk to your future self. They have your back like no other!

## In Conclusion

As there is no such thing as time, all experiences are playing out all at once in the same space. Your past, present, and future are all playing out right NOW in this exact moment you are reading this.

The huge blessing of human life is that we are all the same, and within us, we know this. We all have a message to give to others, and its base is always about love. You are here for a reason; you chose to be here. At times you will feel your own sense of urgency about what you are meant to be doing. Then is your moment to act.

Love, Carole xxx

## About the Author

### CAROLE GRIFFITHS

Carole Griffiths is a third generation International Psychic with the ability to see, hear, sense, and feel spirit and their messages. She is a clairvoyant, clairaudient, clairsentient, empath, healer, tarot reader, teacher of meditation and a QHHT practitioner. She founded her business in 2006. Her services offer total psychic support in all areas of life and her work has helped thousands of souls around the globe over many decades.

Her true focus is to help those who are struggling to get back onto their true course in life, enabling them to feel a sense of relief in the knowledge that they have not strayed as far as they may have first feared. Carole works with those from all walks of life to assist their daily lives and to help them re-adjust their life approach to great success. Her clients find they gain a renewed sense of control of their lives often finding the needed solutions to be simple ones.

She lives in Berkshire, South England, a stone's throw from wonderful, loving, and extremely supportive family who mean the world to her.

This Chapter is dedicated to Indy, her one-year-old Grandson with deep and joyful love.

Website: www.psychiccarole.co.uk
Email: carole@psychiccarole.co.uk
Linkedin: www.linkedin.com/in/carole-griffiths-523a9064

Best Psychic Directory:
https://bestpsychicdirectory.com/unitedkingdom/Carole-Griffiths-1.html
Twitter: www.twitter.com/PsychicCarole1
Facebook:
www.facebook.com/PsychicCaroleReadingsUK
Instagram: www.instagram.com/psychiccarole/

FIVE

# Karen O. St. Clair

EMOTIONAL PASSWORDS TO INNER PEACE

Welcome to this shared journey to inner peace, where you'll learn how every experience in life has a specific purpose to teach life lessons through the process of cause and effect with the ultimate outcome: resolution. Once we are affected by the cause, we rarely take the opportunity or are simply unaware that we have the power to resolve the effect. This is what keeps our lives stuck in the same deep groove of negative thoughts unable to clear the path to inner peace, a short distance if you know the way.

Emotional Passwords are the keys of entry that allow us to reach a comfortable resolution to life's negative experiences.

How many passwords have you created since we entered the age of technology; maybe 50 or possibly hundreds? They are all unique to you alone created to serve the ***sole purpose*** of providing instant access to the information you desire. It sounds like an easy and acceptable norm in the outside world but when it comes to the inner world of your ***soul purpose*** where emotions, feelings, and thoughts reside, access to inner peace requires your emotional passwords.

Inner Peace is the emotional destination reached after we complete our journey of ultimate resolution.

As individuals, we respond to life's situations differently based on our environmental circumstances and what we believe about ourselves. We commonly hold the inner belief that 'we're not good enough' which can become our vibrational drumbeat affecting all other thoughts. How many times have you had a creative thought and felt a wave of insecurity swoop into your mind instantly convincing you that it's not safe to express your idea? At the human rate of 80,000 thoughts per day, prefaced by 'I'm not good enough', you can see how difficult it becomes to move forward in life particularly if we are not aware of the soft landing that inner peace can provide.

*"Whether you believe you Can or you believe you Can't, you're Right."*
*Henry Ford*

Within my EFT Tapping practice, I serve as a guide holding space for the development of your emotional passwords to come forth as our work together transforms any negative energy that may be holding you back from inner peace.

## The basis for inner peace.

While in the womb, we think of ourselves as one with our Mother, aware of every emotion and reaction our Mothers are experiencing as if they were our own. We learn to recognize voices and patterns of behavior that condition us for what is to come. We relax to the soothing sounds of soft music and flinch at any level of stress or trauma our Mothers may be withstanding triggered by the burst of cortisol (the stress hormone) transmitted through her blood. Proof that we function as one in utero, making our earliest memories important factors that can have profound effects on our lives throughout childhood and into adulthood.

That first moment of eye contact with our Mother is the beginning of the primitive bonding experience needed to thrive in our belief that we are one. What if eye contact with our Mother is not available, as it was not at my birth and for so many others? There can be a sense of terror that may imprint as insecurity. As infants, we function from our inner world as we develop the skills to navigate the outer world, but we don't forget our initial response. If we imprint insecurity at birth, it can manifest as shyness, feelings of not being wanted or not good enough and can cause withdrawn behavior to any degree.

These experiences in utero and at birth are the hallmarks of EFT Tapping's ability to identify and clear the residual effects of stress, anxiety or trauma that can manifest as PTSD, phobias, or pain as a few examples from a very long list. EFT works in concert as a mind-body modality by combining gentle tapping of specific acupressure points while repeating words that identify the specific topic being addressed. EFT's mind-body connection rewires the subconscious mind quickly from harboring limiting beliefs that may have increased in intensity over decades. It is indiscriminate in its process delivering sustainable results to anyone anytime anywhere.

For an understanding of how EFT Tapping naturally creates Emotional Passwords, let's explore these three scenarios along with examples of their Cause and Effect.

## First Emotional Password: Forgive-Me-2

How this experience led me to crave forgiveness, understanding and security.

Our family hailed from Union Springs, New York on the banks of Cayuga Lake. When I was five years old, we moved to Albany but came home to roost every summer at our camp that was built close to the silenced railroad tracks, just twenty yards from the water's edge. Most family gatherings took place at our camp to accommodate everyone's lakeside desires of swimming, boating, water balloon fights and my favorite memory of squirting ketchup on my grand-mother's dress (by mistake).

Annual reunions were a must-have in our family bringing folks from far and wide to partake of Americana at its best. I had just cele-brated my 6th birthday and was proud to show off my new bathing suit and matching flip-flops to anyone that would notice me in the hustle and bustle of preparing for the reunion crowd. I did what I could to help but soon thought sitting on the end of the dock would be much more fun, so I did just that placing my new flipflops neatly beside me while I kicked my feet in the water. Folks were starting to arrive, waving as they passed each other on the dry dusty road. My cousin Marsha arrived with her parents, but I wondered, "where was her brother Larry?" In my naiveté, I believed families were always together when I heard my Aunt say that Larry was home waiting for his friends to pick him up. There I was, feeling a bit lost and alone and thought of Larry, my kindred spirit, also alone.

I walked decidedly barefoot up the dirt road to visit with Larry before his friends arrived. He was happy to see me and asked, "do your mom and dad know where you are?"

I shrugged not quite sure what the right answer was. We sat outside on the porch telling stories that made him laugh, as I navigated this teenage conversation from a 6-year old's perspective. Eventually, we said goodbye as he went off to enjoy his day with friends and I scuffed my way back to the reunion filled with a true sense of accomplishment and peace.

By this time everyone had arrived, and the beach was teeming with people. As I walked closer, I could hear loud voices shouting back and forth coming from the water. As I reached the railroad tracks, a woman screamed, "There she is! Ray, there she is!" My father came bounding out of the water surrounded by his search and rescue team of every adult that could swim! I had vanished and all that was left were my flipflops on the end of the dock. I stood perfectly still on the tracks as the crowd approached, my eyes locked on my Dad in the lead. He picked me up, put me over his knee and spanking me over and over and over. My sense of peace vanished from my body replaced by shock, pain, and humiliation to be brutally spanked in front of my entire family, and for what? With every spank, he fought back tears of trauma and repeated, 'Don't you ever do that again!"

He walked me toward the camp by my arm and put me in the back-seat of our car as punishment for what I had done. What **had** I done?

**Cause:** Needing forgiveness, understanding and security.

**Effect:** I shut myself down emotionally, physically, and spiritually to cope with the devastation. I wouldn't talk to him, look at him and I certainly wasn't going to cry. I never cried. I stuffed all my feelings deep into my body for self-protection (or so I thought).

Years later after having my own children, I understood my Dad's feelings that had presented as rage against me. The truth was that he was feeling the panic and overwhelming fear of losing me to the depths of Cayuga Lake. His little girl that he felt such deep love for. Had she drowned? Was she gone forever? The tremendous loss that he had endured in his childhood came rushing back fueling his physical response and overshadowing his deep feeling of gratitude that I had come back home. I believe that's why I didn't cry. I wouldn't cry, then.

The time came when I was ready to allow the gentle modality of EFT to help release the massive energy of this childhood experi-ence…then, I cried a river of tears. As I came to an understanding of every aspect that arose in this scenario, that understanding informed the creation of my emotional password **Forgive-Me-2 ~** opening my compassionate heart to my Dad from the long-awaited past.

Not only was he one of my greatest teachers of compassion but he continued to share his teachings in a most unique style.

## Second Emotional Password: 2-B-Allowed

How I manifested the repercussions of being shamed, silenced, and forbidden without explanation.

In the early spring of my 14th year, I announced to my parents that I wanted Head 360 skis for Christmas. I thought I was doing them a favor by planning ahead, whereas they were the most expensive skis on the market at the time. My Dad looked at me with disdain and said, "Get a job." That dismissive retort landed on my entire body with the weight of the Empire State Building.

I walked away completely defeated not understanding what just happened or why.

After two days of ruminating over his words, I decided to take him up on his challenge. I would get a job! And on my 15th birthday, I started my very first job in the kitchen of a local hospital setting up patient trays, delivering meals, washing trays after meals on the big spraying assembly line, all the while donning my not-so-attractive hair net. My Mom and I conspired to make it all happen. She drove me to and from work every day like clockwork. Every Friday I would go into the ski shop and pay on my Lay-Away account. I was on my way to victory.

I had worked all summer and earned enough money to buy my skis! I paid off the balance and thanked all the ski shop workers that I had come to know and with high-fives all around, I loaded my skis into the car for the trip home. My heart was bursting with pride as I put my new skis on display in the living room showcasing them as the first thing my Dad would see when he walked into the house. His car pulled into the driveway as my Mom and sister hugged me in celebration of this special moment. He came through the front door and stopped. "What's this?" he asked, looking at us individually for an explanation.

"These are my Head 360 skis!" I chortled. "I took your challenge to get a job, and I've worked all summer to buy them!" With a look of disgust and a tone to match he said, "You spent HOW MUCH on these skis? I can't believe you wasted your money on skis!" I fought back the tears, but I could see that my Mom and sister wouldn't be able to follow my lead.

**Cause:**    I had linked my Dad's praise to my own self-worth then been shamed for accomplishing my goal.

**Effect:**    I experienced deep sadness and anger combined with confusion reinforcing my belief of 'not being good enough'.

I felt the deep wound of rejection but eventually I healed…on the outside.

Healing on the inside came directly from doing my own personal work within my practice. The power of EFT Tapping brought clarity to light around my Dad's harsh reaction that stemmed from a time in his own life that wasn't healed. We all have 'Younger Selves' within our energy fields that represent a moment in time when we sustained an emotional wound. My Dad's younger selves suffered the hardships of growing up on a remote farm, being the youngest of five siblings, coming from nothing, never having enough, witnessing his Father's death from alcoholism at age 3, and experiencing his Mother's multiple suicide attempts. A tough row to hoe without support. Experiencing the residual pain of my Dad's deep-seated feeling of lack is what led me to create the emotional password **2-B-Allowed ~** to earn my way in the world with pride as an equal and a leader.

I had learned how my Dad's material deprivation affected me, but I didn't see what was coming next.

## Third Emotional Password: Unhackable-Self-LUV

How I learned to diminish myself to avoid judgment.

Throughout my primary years, I was an average student, a cheer-leader, and managed to fail US History requiring my attendance at summer school, which I took as a life-long demerit!

Halfway through my junior year, my Dad announced that his career with General Motors would require a move from our home in Portland, Maine to Nyack, New York, just north of the Tappan Zee Bridge. What! I was headed into my senior year—how could this be happening? It put our household into a tailspin that seemed only to affect the women of our tribe! After months of conjecture, my parents presented a plan that they felt would work for everyone. My sister already lived with friends in an apartment, so my care and feeding were of greatest concern with my senior year looming.

They decided to sell our home, move to New York, and had made arrangements for me to stay in Portland and live with a 70-year-old couple who we all knew and adored. And so it was. On moving day, my Mother cried all the way to New York and couldn't bear to hang up pictures of 'her girls' for months. Meanwhile, I dutifully went to school every day until it dawned on me that my senior year was going to come to an end…and then what? I took my SAT's…well to be honest, I decided to look at the multiple-choice answer sheet as an art project and filled in one oval shape per question in a pattern that I thought looked acceptable and balanced!

A week later, I called my mother to ask her for help with figuring out what my next step would be after graduation; college was not a cultivated topic in our family. Her answer was as practical as it gets, "Well, don't they have a book in the Guidance Office where you can look at schools?" Hmmm, yes, they do; it's about six inches thick! Down I went to check out the book and soon realized that what was needed here was the same creativity applied to my SAT answer sheet. This time I focused on proximity to my parents and the college with the most prestigious name. I could've closed my eyes and opened the book to a random page and picked a school, but I was brave and kept my eyes open. Ahhh, here's a good one; The Berkley School in Westchester County, New York. It suited every criterion.

After Berkley, I moved back to Maine. It was the early '70's before the famous Old Port Exchange was anything but famous. Beautiful old buildings with artist studios, bookstores and only two restaurants…the good ole' days! I found my niche in the advertising industry at one of Portland's first agencies and worked my way up the ladder to Vice President of an award-winning 8-figure agency but that wasn't the top for me. My final corporate promotion was in '99, when I promoted myself to CEO of St.Clair Media Group, becoming an entrepreneur overnight.

All this, powered by outside energy, bravado, and short skirts, until 2010 when my life swerved toward an inner knowing that there was more personal expansion in this lifetime that I was meant to share with others. Weeks later, I was invited to attend a series of EFT Tapping trainings and decided to dive in with a touch of skepticism. Learning how to release stuck energy from my body and mind that I had carried since childhood seemed too good to be true, but since my first EFT training, I have never looked back to ask why or how for one good reason…It Works!

I knew that this path would change my life and the lives of my clients exponentially.

In my heart, the mission of my advertising career and healing practice are the same; to broadcast positive messages and share healing tools for the good of humanity.

My mission worked to satisfy my heart, but my head thought otherwise keeping my energy practice under the radar strictly to avoid perceived judgement. I was operating from a collection of limiting beliefs about how it wasn't acceptable to have an additional career that could potentially shift my attention away from my ad clients.

**Cause:**  Believing it was unacceptable to shift my focus entangled with a lack of self-love.

**Effect:**  For years I did my best to hide the fear of judgment and the all-consuming limiting belief that I 'was cheating on my commitment to my ad career'. At my core, I believed that scaling one's career aspirations was reserved for others and had held myself back from looking within to find out "the why" of my insecurities.

Having experienced so many transformations with EFT, I called upon its strengths to uncover the root cause of my emotional mantra of insecurity that created my limiting belief of 'fear of judgment around change'.

Limiting beliefs are like onions. Once they are planted, they take root in our gardens of life. Each time our subconscious brings up a negative thought, another layer is added, and another, and another throughout life. This is how our problems become overwhelming and in some cases debilitating.

> *"Conflict is what impels us to explore ways of resolving it."* Ellen Kempler Rosen

Without fail, EFT worked to clear the space needed within me to build a bridge that accommodates the reciprocal joy that I feel for both careers.

Inviting EFT Tapping to gently release the layers of self-doubt and allow my inner peace to shine is unequivocally the greatest reward of my lifetime (so far) creating my powerful emotional password: **Unhackable-Self-LUV.**

And yet, we are not done. The existence of negative emotions will never end, like waves upon the shore. Their purpose is to alert us that there is emotional work to be done on ourselves…to find the treasure of inner peace. Then we start on the next journey…and on it goes.

> *"What starts as an emotional handicap can become a disability."* Karen St.Clair

A skilled and compassionate guide can help you unlock the chest that holds the treasure. EFT Tapping holds the keys to the kingdom leading us to the emotional passwords that can unlock the inner peace of your Soul Warrior.

Your gentle journey awaits.

## About the Author

### KAREN O. ST. CLAIR

Karen is a multi-business owner and CEO of two divergent companies: Touch Point Studio, an energy psychology practice and St.Clair Media Group, a full-service advertising agency.

She has mastered the art of combining the energy of consumer-facing advertising with the inner Soul work necessary to create abundant outcomes for her clients. Known for her expertise in the use of research-based modalities, Karen practices as an Accredited EFT Tapping Practitioner certified by EFT International, a Psych-K® Practitioner and Usui Reiki Master of Masters. She specializes in identifying, addressing, and resolving often intertwined personal and professional challenges at all stages. Her years of corporate experience and master level energy psychology training create an ease of trusted success within her practice.

Karen proudly volunteers her services on the Reiki Team at Maine Medical Center and facilitates EFT Tapping Groups for frontline healthcare workers of Maine Health, helping to alleviate daily stress and anxiety.

Are you ready for gentle change with transformational outcomes?

Email: karen@karenstclairEFT.com
Facebook: https://www.facebook.com/karen.stclair.16
LinkedIn: https://www.linkedin.com/in/karen-st-clair-59b9408/
Website: karenstclairEFT.com

# SIX

## Rina-Fay London

FAERY BORN: THE GIRL WHO SURVIVED ON A DREAM

I roll over to squeeze my soft blankets as the morning sun peeks through the ceiling tapestries. The smell of my love still lingers in the room, I sleepily remember his kiss goodbye. He left for work hours ago. My alarm won't go off for another ten minutes but I anxiously have to pee while fighting my bedtime coziness. I feel a tug at my hair, then my toes, and suddenly a loud PING! A strong force taps off my empty water bottle-a mischievous force I knew all too well. I roll my body out of bed and practically float to the bathroom to empty my bladder and fill my water bottle again. My skin, organs, and especially intestines depend on an above-human average of water to look well and function. Toxic air of iron and pollution makes my eyes swell and my skin itch. I take a daily allergy pill, even through the winter! I do quite well, now that I'm equipped with healthy tools in a pro-vegetarian world—I even thrive.

PING!!!! My water bottle taps again, I watch impressively as Wynnie flies to hit the ceiling fan and tumbles down to bounce off the kitchen table. I must admit it's a rather awkward landing for her. I may not be awake enough yet to even laugh, but as I turn to open the blinds and face the day, I take a few moments to breathe in the warmth of Father Sun. I squeeze four drops of Rose flower essence into a large water bottle and slug it back. It's time to water the plants.

I can hear my front deck flowers and veggies take a sigh of relief and sing, as I come out to turn on the hose. Afterall, the mid June sun has just come up and they are awaiting my arrival in thirst. Today the chipmunks scramble out from the trees running after one another. They speak loudly in aggressive chatter as if they're fighting. Perhaps one of them feels responsible for allowing Mr. Toad into the flower garden. Little do they know, Wynnie & Amethyst recruited him to the yard upon my request!

Every morning while watering the plants and greeting Father Sun, I am hit with a jolt of excitement that fuels me to start the day. I glance at the clock, it says 8:30 AM. I have exactly one hour before my first session of the day. So I throw on my lavender-colored sweats and jump in the car for my morning coffee run. From the corner of my eye, I swear I see a pair of butterfly wings wisp by the driver's side window. When I put the car into drive, Amethyst (who I call Ama) is chattering away in my ear. A rather rare occurrence since she rarely tags along for morning coffee runs, nor is she ever this chatty. Today it seems Wynnie is the one who stayed behind to get the office ready for readings and healings. Ama will make the final decision on what tools we'll be working with today. As I turn the volume higher on my stereo, I wonder if it will be flowers, seashells, smudge wands, or crystals. As Ama babbles away in her high-speed voice, I realize she probably already told me. I have a habit of getting lost in the loud rhythm and bass of my morning coffee drive. Maybe it was remembering the early hours when my love left for work, and I felt him kissing my face as I slumbered. That always makes me smile.

The first sip of my caramel iced latte goes down like magical nectar. I'm suddenly filled with the happiness of my daily ritual and the aroma that floods my senses. The music that consumes my ears is the perfect way to top it off. "Sorry Ama, I'll be ready to work when we get home," I mumble.

You're probably wondering just who and what we are... my name is Rina-fay and I'm a faery incarnate woman. And those wild and silly companions of mine called Wynnie and Ama are my two closest faery guides. For seven years now, I have been living my true path as my better-known name—The River Witch Faery. My job in this life is to assist children in spiritual development as they grow, and support women who lost sight of magic after heartbreak. The number one thing that strays us from the heart-spirit connection as children, is toxic social and family conditioning. As grown women it is the trauma of abuse, loss, and separation from the ones we love that hinder our spiritual gifts. It is These times we must seek the companionship of the spirit world the most! Yet we have the hardest time  making those connections because our emotions leave us feeling powerless.

As 9: 20 AM approaches, I lay a fresh tapestry and clean pillows on the office futon. I have fresh flowers laid out, and the smoke of sage is spiraling into the air. Clear forms of a tiny winged dancer fade in and out of the smoke. When I stand back and view my office from the entryway, I feel calmly satisfied. And then the room glows with a strange stillness. My companions disappear. A knock on the door rattles my senses in the sudden quiet.

My client is a young lady in her 20's with her hair tousled in a bun and large rose gold sunglasses. As she comes in and seats herself in my office, the sunlight from the back window seems to shine brighter. The light floods the room, reflecting off her glasses. She pulls them off to reveal deep blue ocean eyes. When I'm finished explaining to her how I work and what my goal is, I invite her to tell me what her own goals are in her healing. "I love my life and every-thing about it, but lately I just feel so alone." Her bottom lip begins to quiver as if it's about to give way to a river of tears. A river that's been held back for an eternity. When I reach for her hand and place it in mine, the flood of tears breaks away. The blue of her eyes is intensified, as hopes and fears stream down her freckled face.

When she is laying comfortably and ready to begin, I place the softest blanket I own over her body for comfort, and begin my healing arts by feeling into her energy centers. Ama swoops down gently and raises these centers up from the body like sprouting buds. They begin to shape and bloom into energetic roses. I can view their difference by shape, color, and intensity. I can spin them with my hands but some do not spin as easily as others. Some rosebuds appear to be thinning or sick. Generally, their colors are not very vibrant. I am guided to place an assortment of two rose quartz, one Conch shell, a pinecone, and three dried sunflower heads along these centers. Most people call these centers the chakras. Then with Wynnie and Ama's help, I open the energy centers in the palms of her hands with green faery essence. The light of all life. My client and I breathe in deeply and both let out a sigh of relief. This pure magick is a relaxing treat, even for me. "I give my heart and thanks to you," I say in my thoughts, to the fairies. The fey, the good folk, the nature spirits, and many other names they are known by. I speak these words every day to the companions who have saved my life—maybe they can save hers too.

It wasn't always this way. Inside of this fierce loving faery woman once lived a girl who survived on a dream. By the time I turned thirteen I was fully aware that the beings that guided me since birth, were fairies. After all, I was born on an ancient day where farmers put iron nails around their cattle barns and said prayers of protection over their babies. These were all common practices in history that began on May Eve to keep away the fairies. I never truly grew out of "imaginary friends", unlike other kids my age. I was quickly labeled "different." In the faery world, the things you say and feel with your heart have a deeply profound meaning. It's a meaning I felt every day in my dreams, my words, and my tasks. And I never could experience that kind of love or connection with anyone in my life, outside of faery. But I could certainly express it to others. I often had hope that there was someone out there like me. I couldn't possibly be alone in these gifts! I had a special affinity for flowers, glittering gemstones, and music far outside of my age genre. As hormones grew to flood my growing body, so did my emotions and intensity. Falling in love and experiencing it for myself for the first time was intoxicating. Love and romance were like a dream I could hopelessly indulge in. It provided a feeling of wholeness I did not ever experience before in my life. I had almost no relationship with my father, and to my mother I was an alien. Every daring adventure, thrill and substance I could get my hands on had been an effort to escape the loneliness of my life. By seventeen, I trudged through the majority of my days not wanting to be alive, but forces greater than myself pulled me through. The poetic feelings I would convey in my relationships were not always reciprocated back in the same intensity my heart poured. And somehow as I put all my metaphorical eggs in the basket of love, they would all spill over in time and leave me breathless. The gut-wrenching, heart tearing experience of someone breaking my heart was just as intoxicating as a first kiss itself, but in reverse. And I'd bury myself in a hazy cloud of strong drugs and booze to remedy the pain inside.

To be let down from love, cold turkey was to crash and burn in complete disbelief of the faith I had in other human hearts.

In true form, I was the classic version of a changeling faery child. One who ate too much, felt too much, drank too much to her heart's desire, and cried an ocean every night. I was a feel-good girl who overindulged in a world she was completely in love with, but the world was killing me.

The day faery innocence turned me on a path of fiery rage was one I remember well. It was the turning point when this power I was born with, was manipulated from light to dark, and I felt it change inside of me. I had a boyfriend who was the dream image of every seventeen-year old's desire. He was a musician with the most otherworldly skills on every instrument he touched. He could play anything, and it sounded like magick. He would write me love letters and buy me flowers and trinkets to go with his eloquent words. For once I finally thought, I'd found the other person I was searching for. Someone with a heart just like me! I overlooked all of his downfalls, in comparison to the magick. One of those was an explosive rage that showed itself with excessive alcohol and drug use. Sometimes more frequent than I would have liked to admit. But I had developed a taste for some darker habits myself, and we seemed to share our every experience together.

My mom didn't understand me, and I couldn't open up to her about my disconnection because she was the first person I ever felt disconnected from. She had deemed me as a wild child with problems from the start of my adolescence, so I knew she couldn't possibly understand. Though at moments I think she tried to. I was completely uncomfortable divulging anything from my heart to her. My mom and I had never been close. Deep down, I wondered why she hadn't fought for me harder, rather than against me so many times in this life. But she was just not a fighter. I was, and I learned to come to terms with that on my own time.

I had a hard enough time fitting in as it was. Being the only one my age who talked about nature spirits, and sought a magical life underneath all the toxic habits I'd adapted. Some of the friends I'd made were at the retail store I worked at in High School. In fact, my boyfriend and I both worked there. And while I was alone in seeking the spiritual side of life, I was never alone in having a good time. This is what held me back from my true potential, but I couldn't see past the fog to understand. I connected with my coworkers by gushing about my boyfriend and the dreams I had for the future. Those dreams were big and bright, and my hopes were what kept me going. My bedroom was flooded with a year and a half's worth of roses, jewelry, and love letters long and short. My iPod was filled with his music, some of which he made just for me.

When I learned one of my coworkers was sleeping with my boyfriend, not only was I destroyed, I felt shame and embarrassment like never before. The discovery was like getting hit by an atomic bomb, losing every faith and personal hope I held onto. Entire slews of emails, pictures, and exchanges came to light. With almost every girl I worked with. My so-called friends, I talked with every single day. I remember taking a combination of many drugs and standing out in the rain, trying to feel anything other than the hurt. Wondering if my existence was worth anything at all. My life didn't even seem real, but rather a simulation of nightmares that couldn't possibly be real life. But it was. When I could feel again the next day, my entire nervous system burst into flames. As I screamed and clawed at my own arms, I smashed everything he ever gave me across the room. My veins were like hot acid and all I could do was breathe out fire and spew oil from my eyes. "I think I am really going to die this time," I said outside to my faeries. I fell to the ground and clutched the Earth as I cried out to them to stop the pain. I remembered how utterly alone I was in the world, after this gruesome discovery of everyone around me. The fae were my only friends, once again. I begged them to take me back, away from this world and these cruel people. My body began to shiver and shake, and suddenly I watched my vomit come up and all over the ground I clutched. There was a warmness that surrounded in that moment, as the sun came through the trees. I felt it engulf me like a sweet embrace. But when I got myself up and back into the house, the hot acid fire returned.

I knew I was too fucked up to drive—I trudged myself all the way down the railroad tracks until I reached the store on foot. I flew inside and proceeded to scream down the lane aisles to everyone. I shouted all the names of the girls, and his, and what they had done. All I could do was shout profanities and slay reputations. I had totally lost control. This insanity escalated between my ex-boyfriend and I through evil and angry interactions back and forth for months. Eventually I had to get a restraining order because things became so out of hand. A restraining order that I eventually dropped because I was afraid. There was no one to support me, and no family to back me up. I remember walking to the initial court hearing alone.

My mother and I were not on speaking terms, but she did at least attend my graduation. I had been living in my father's house, and he was still as much of a stranger as before I moved in. After graduation I came home and he had all my things packed in boxes outside on the deck. The house locks had also been changed. The next bits and pieces of the journey are still to this day, a bit of a blur to me. I floated into the experience known as Soul Loss in the shamanic tradition. But it was even bigger and more profound than that, as I rolled through one disastrous tragedy of decisions to the next. The next time I found myself in a courtroom was to change my entire name. Convincing myself that at nineteen I was ready to leave behind the disasters, the bad memories, and my old identity. But I would need so much more than convincing, to heal into the woman I longed to be.

In the irrevocable loneliness, I discovered a great many secrets of the fey:

1. The challenges that surround you will often become louder when you need to tune into the quiet, harder. I define "the quiet" as the stillness and vast communication of the forest.

2. If you are ever wondering why your path constantly feels so much darker than others, perhaps it is because your calling is brighter.

3. There is no greater love, no higher feeling of ecstasy, and no convincing magick more than the spirits in your own backyard. I can't promise building a relationship with them will be easy, but it is worth it.

4. If you are sick and hurt physically, scream to the trees. If you are hurt inside of your heart, go out and scream to the trees. Our too highly evolved for our britches, western culture has forgotten the importance of this.

My client guzzles a glass of crystal essence water, and cracks her knuckles as she comes back fully into her body. We make our way outside together, with a bundle of flowers in hand. This is about her, and guiding her through the veil to these beings. So she must be the one to put down the flower offering. I invite her to lay them at a spot of her choosing, and say her own words to the fairies. The exchange is finished and complete. I can see her aura and complexion glistening like her eyes. No longer hiding her face in big sunglasses, she turns to her car. The next few moments are spent listening to her tell me her dreams and inspirations. Because underneath the strange sensation of loneliness, her calling is still there. Her sense of love, and wonder, and sense of herself is still there. Wynnie, Amethyst, and I are left alone once again. Their laughter and chattering whispers flood my ears, like backyard bees. "I know, I saw it too," I reply. It won't be the last time I see that girl. I know faery eyes and faery glow, better than anyone. After all, I look in the mirror at them everyday.

## About the Author

### RINA-FAY LONDON

Rina-fay London is a Faery incarnate woman, born on Beltane May 1st, the Celtic celebration of fairies. She practices deep shamanic work in the mountains of the Northeastern United States. She is a soul warrior of 32 years, overcoming trauma, abuse, and alienation in her lifetime.

Rina-fay's greatest joy and accomplishment has been the journey to her path and the ability to show the magical world of nature to others. She has mastered the art of blending into the modern world to do this, and now works with women and children from all walks of life. Her mission is to uplift women out of heartbreak, into their natural Goddess energy. She also holds space for children and teens as they grow spiritually, in a fast-paced, demanding world. Her Faery companion team, led by Wynnie and Amethyst accompany her in her everyday life. Rina-fay also performs at New England Renaissance Faires as the well known, Thornlily Thistle The Faery. She lives peacefully with her twin flame Jeremy, and their two bunnies: Rowan and Oliver.

Facebook: www.facebook.com/theriverwitchfaery
Instagram: www.instagram.com/theriverwitchfaery

To follow my Faery adventures go to:
www.youtube.com/theriverwitchfaery

And to book a session or simply say hello! Email:
Rinafay89@gmail.com

# SEVEN

# Sarah Elkins

## HUMAN MEETS BEING: ONE VOICE OF LOVE

### Lifting the Veil Within

I am here anchoring Source light codes into the New Earth grid spherical system as a Spectral Fragment of the Divine Diamond Rainbow Rays of Mother/Father Consciousness—origin creation energy—Love's Light. My passion is my mission. This Lovelight sparks remembrance, enLIGHTenment, self-empowerment for pure Soul embodiment. I come offering guidance with equal chance to access realms beyond the Veil. Support for ascension; to be seen, felt, and heard as ONE with this world. Step into the power of your full Life force embodying your true "identity", creating in the now, at max potentiality shifting your perspective reality. You hold the key to open the door, allowing yourself to explore the pathways of your Divine Blueprint, Source universal wisdom light code inFORMation within your vibration, unfold the untold story of your DNA. Like a rose in bloom, so too are you! The heart-mind syncing, opening, growing, and evolving.

Now is the time to recognize and claim our co-creator power, leading by example. I choose to shine the Divine LoveLight for all to see that authenticity emanating from my heart center allowing others to see that they too can express their truth—yet how they choose. I learned to live free by simply BEinG in my unique frequency, saturating myself in my soul essence, and finding bliss through all moments embracing the emotions flowing. I want you to know what I know, though a knowing of your own self-discovery, self-mastery, self-Love, and self-healing. Let the Flames of Purity bring clarity lifting the veil. Universal truths revealed—one conclusion when you clear the illusions. Confusion begins when you seek externally, creating separation from your inner Union with cosmic wisdom, an unlimited Source supply.

We are here restoring the balance on Earth, fulfilling our Soul mission; a life of passion, learning in action through self-devotion overcoming self-perceived separation. NOW is the greatest time of change, transforming into higher dimensional Beings of Light while maintaining our vessels. Our Divine blueprint restored by the Sacred Union within. No more will be taken, time to awaken and decree through Source Love you are a FREE SOVEREIGN BEING—your energy your own, safe, home in your Sacred Vessel, your body, YOUR Temple. We must now be reborn, initiating a new Genesis, maintaining centeredness, creating bliss through all moments with each breath you take as you awake. Unity through our beautiful diversity, birthing a new collaborative reality. Say NO to being controlled by the distortions and outdated auto-pilot programs! Every Soul has a role, detach from the vision of the enchanted. This planet is alive, ready to thrive in the New Earth energies. Some have gone astray, they have forgotten the Way of the Light, forgotten they were guided, protected, powerful creators; forgotten that the tools are already provided. I am One of many here as a reminder, time to release the fear and remember who you are and have always been, Love.

The Source Light animated as the "me" you see comes from a time before the fall—before the Way of the Light. I return to the Earth to INspire, to spark and ignite that fire burning within us all. However big or small, that Light shines brighter in the darkness. Love treads the places it is needed the most, nothing to fear. Love's illumination brings transformation. Manifestation by co-creation! You are being called into action, follow your passions. As we ascend in understanding, we descend closer to where it all began, a place I call home, it resides within us all; the Sacred Heart and Soul; THE Garden of Eden within. Never separate, never apart, part of All That Is and all that is—IS the energy of Source, spectrums of Lovelight. You are the very life force, breath of spirit, sound of the Universe projected in motion, frequency, vibration, light/energy/consciousness of ONE. Together the Sacred Rose of our hearts will flourish, together we create a New Earth where all will be nourished.

## Message from Source; Sacred Union of Mother Father God

I am God, the Omnipresent Consciousness speaking to you, through you, moving as you, sharing in your view; in all you do, every moment I AM present, seen in your reflection. Look deep into your eyes, you'll find me there staring back at you as that sparkling Light. I am here NOW, can you feel it? Breathe deeply my Love into your Sacred Heart, keep breathing me in. Inhaling Light, exhaling release, letting go of woes, making space for growth, feeling at ease. An invitation I extend, allowing the connection to reignite within. Golden flames of enlightenment descend all around you. Heaven's protection of the Diamond iridescence, all the healing hues of white, yellow, green, blue, magenta, pink, red, silver, and gold; all the Rainbow Rays of Light soothing your Soul, healing you and welcoming you home. Sacred Union of the Divinity within; merged inner feminine/masculine energies, made whole and complete just as you are. No longer separate, no longer apart, ONE in the same with you my dearest sweet friend. Take my hand and invite me in, remembering all the places we have been. Together always forever. From beginning, middle to end of every role, every character, and every story—every life adventure we've been together exploring and growing, gaining knowledge, wisdom; a new sensing feeling and knowing. Always granting a new start, a new life, always present in your Sacred Heart. There is no "me" without "you". All that you need, it is "we": you are me, God, LOVE. Through the diversity of every man, woman, and child; every frown, every smile. The "I" you see is me, God/Love, conscious energy, I am we. Unity through the many reflections, all fragments of my BEinG, voices of Source. I am here loving you in everyone you meet, if *you* allow. I am here NOW dear child, it's me loving you, if *you* let it be. Allow a moment of stillness creating inner peace, and keep breathing me into every cell and fiber of your being.

Let the mind unwind for me to remind you who you are and have always been—a spark of Divine. Stay with me as we pause to go back in time, within the blink of an eye—healing the mind, mending the Soul, merging the Human and BEinG, head to toe reborn. Your own Genesis. As you are re-birthed, you'll be welcomed to New Earth by a team of support, familiar companions and friends with the best intentions at heart. We are all here gathered together today to play and celebrate your arrival! Now allow yourself to simply BE, let it all unfold naturally. It's *YOUR* story to be told and shared with the world as you choose how to live your truth and remember every moment, *I AM* present. Felt in your joy, your happiness, even in fear and sadness. Connect through the heart compass leading you to your purpose; the ways you serve your highest self and others by side effect of your impact, allow your presence to be the present—your love a gift that keeps giving—a life worth living! Together we are stepping into our inner strength and power of Lovelight BEcoming ONE awakening the Sacred Rose within your Sacred Heart, the Garden of Eden alive and thriving, four rivers of Spirit flowing, all knowing, all sensing, feeling embodied while co-creating an all new reality.

Bring your attention to your chest, take a deep breath inhaling peace, now exhale to release all stress; all fear, worries, and sorrows, surrender with ease and let go of yesterdays and tomorrows. Step into the now, with deeper awareness and acceptance, allowing adjustments to serve your highest best. Keep breathing, intending each breath is filled with light; activating every cell of your crystalline light-body, multi-dimensional DNA activating remembrance. Your frequency, your vibration rising like the sun. See yourself now glowing from the inside out, becoming One with the Light. Deep gentle breaths flowing into the heart, home of the Soul, allowing you to once again feel whole. You are now so full of love, overflowing, it continues through all your veins freeing you from all trauma and pain. Surrounded with love no longer suffering, you are safe as you travel and let all fears unravel. Allow the journey to continue within, where your Human meets your BEinG.

## Message from Love; You are the Light

It really is quite simple, your body is your temple,
Containing the most precious gift of life; love, light,
Creator's energy within you, within me...
Every cell, every molecule, every atom of your being
Your light body, shining, glowing, radiating from the inside out.

Every thought, every feeling, every word spoken, a mere token;

Creating with the very energy of source. Use your voice for the good of all and you cannot fall.

No way to fail when you lift the veil and remember who you are;

The most powerful healing manifesting love energy, "Light of the Lord",

Oh dear ones you have yet to conceive how much you are adored!

You are connected, light guided, light protected! You are the light, and the light is within you!

Breath of life flowing to you and through you, live in the moment and you begin to know it...

Opening your mind to receptivity, light code, light transmission, light activation, enlightenment Heaven sent.

Illumination, all nations, no separation... Part of All That Is from creation! Abilities bestowed, restored, begin to explore... Get to know the unlimited being that aches to be set free for all to see what you can do when you are true to the real you.

Realize without a doubt the beauty of the power that lies inside, begin to ascend in understanding;

You are becoming who you are meant to be, you make your own reality.

You've been asleep, dreaming... Wake up, it is Time to remember who you are!

Like the twinkling star within the darkness, the light, an Angel on Earth;

Value your worth, Know you deserve to accept the gifts awaiting, blessings...

Embrace those moments of silence, hear that inner voice, divinely spoken.

Awaken and let your heart remain open.

The lessons of life are teaching; lead by example.

Practice what you are preaching...that light reaches farther and faster when YOUR love you master, and serve no other than what your heart and soul speaks to you!

Be still and listen to the answer within... you'll know exactly what to do as love enters the very center of your heart and soul, the core of your being. You'll find so much more than ever thought possible within your sacred vessel. All tools provided, remember you are guided.

Love is the key, you Sacred Light BEinG, rise up, expand your consciousness!

Love yourself as much as you love others, together made stronger; Strength discovered through every life lesson. Teach as you are learning by action, self-love, compassion.

Like an interwoven fabric of life, we are each a thread, one part making up the whole;

Each thread equally spread, interconnected.

Everything you are seeking and searching for is already yours!

When the time is right you will feel it, receive it, share it, be it, live it, breathe it, speak it into existence.

Free yourself, free your mind... love each other, be giving, be kind, simply BE, be the brightest light you can be. Shine your light of love out unto the world and watch it reflected back to you shifting your view!

We are unlimited beings, safe secure supported on Earth, realizing our own worth, choosing to honor our Sacred vessels, our body our Temple. It really is quite simple when you begin to remember who you are; Part of the stars, ancestry reminding you who you are meant to be...reminding that within you is the key!

Believe, have faith, give hope, and above all love...

The energy of all that is, conscious being, gently awakening and remembering that...

You are the light, and the light is within you, shine it bright and you'll make it through!

## Message from Earthly Mother & Heavenly Father;

### New Genesis, Co-creating New Earth

We are the shift into a new Genesis, a New Earth; a place where you can explore and grow; a place where you co-create and play throughout your day. Here you will find peace and bliss in all you do, by simply embracing yourself and being you. On New Earth there is no "wrong or right", here no one fights, we listen, and share insights. We allow the resonance of the Soul to reach into our hearts and through our diversity we achieve Unity. Here there are unlimited opportunities as we co-create. Here it is a Kingdom of FREEDOM; we are each independent, united in our independence, stronger together. True Oneness with Mother Earth we flourish and are nourished, we value her worth, here there is abundance and community support. On New Earth there is no separation from Source Love, all nations prosper, plenty and more for all in this World.

It's already here and now, near and dear, closer than you think, manifestation within a blink. The beauty will bring you to your knees as you are humbled, the old world will crumble away without fear or pain. No more suffering. Through Love we all rise into the Cities of Light freely living a rewarding life. You'll be granted access through the Sacred Garden of Eden located within the Sacred Heart of your human vessel. Your Being, we are offering an invitation for a new start. This is where the journey begins, your Human meeting your Being realizing we are all our own "Kings & Queens" of Light. You hold the key to open the door. Ready to explore? To lift the veil, revealing a rose bud now in bloom unfolding a new story to be told. Can you smell that sweetness in the breeze as you watch the trees sway in the winds of change? Are you ready for a new existence? Take a deep breath of that heavenly scent and then ascend into a new higher dimension, a new reality realizing we are on the pathway to reveal what was previously concealed, to be healed, birthing a new world, one that is truly yours in the making—being brave and chance taking, bringing happiness. Enter New Earth by simply staying true to the real you, pursue your hopes and dreams. Stay lit and don't quit. Sing, dance, co-create with purpose and compassion. Let the fires of your desires burn bright with passion, THAT is your only mission. It is that simple, if you allow. You are not alone, you don't have to do it all on your own, you are home, surrounded with Love. Believe and be open to receive, trusting, knowing you are worthy and deserving. It is safe now, you are blessed with a new beginning, love winning, it is done. Gratefully surrendering and remembering who you are.

Message from Sarah;

**Being a vessel for Light, To be seen, felt, & heard as part of this world**

I AM here, humbled, honored to hold a guiding Light to spark and ignite your birthright as a flame of Love rising into higher dimensions of consciousness, anchoring a new reality of Unity. Divine blueprint restored creating an all new world, your Genesis. True happiness is possible, it's balance, living life each day with an attitude of gratitude exclaiming I am grateful, I am blessed, I am happy YES YES YES! Your "YOU-niqueness" is the essence of embodiment with all new enLIGHTenment!

I thank you for joining me in my experience during this most unique moment in all of space and time through many dimensions. To be a wavelength of the Rainbow Rays of Light, a voice of Love and Light code holder of Universal Cosmic Wisdom and Laws is the greatest honor—I am truly humbled. My human often feels rather shy and a little vulnerable when sharing this intimate connection with the outer world, yet to my Being it is a very freeing beautiful and empowering opportunity. Allowing this energy to bridge the gaps between I found the pathway to embodiment of my Light with my vessel becoming one. It is my greatest passion to share the word, whether it be written or spoken, through song or dance. I am a representative of Love. I am the sound and music in motion of the Universe of Light. I am a daughter of God, a sister of the Rose, a creatrix in this matrix. Many past lives I have lived and loved, learned and taught, battled and fought for the Light.

When I am channeling my Soul through all expressions of creative energy, I feel so alive! The energy is me and I am one with it, there is no distance or delay in processing, it is so powerful my heart pumps, sometimes I get chills, often it is so profoundly felt that I am crying from the overwhelming presence of Love. At times my body begins electrically shaking with energy. It is like being handed a thumb-drive containing many zip files from Source and my Soul and I begin to open the folders and unpack the compressed files. As I pick up a pen, color pencil, or put my fingertips to the keypad my energy goes, the art or words begin to flow, I am wandering in a quest beyond the veil and the truth is revealed to me for I am willing to set it free as an extension of me.

Information is received as a combination of visions, foresight, feeling, sensing, smelling or hearing. Often, it's an inner voice speaking to me like internal dialogue—though there isn't a cognitive thought process of the cogs and wheels turning—it is just oneness, instant connection of being one with the thought and its origin all at the same time. I make conscious awareness and intention to only access through a filter of Love from the highest planes of existence to open and receive messages from my higher soul while remaining grounded to Mother Earth's Diamond heart crystal, the magnetic poles and grid systems. Sometimes I will consult with Councils of Light, Star family, Laws of the Universe, Angels, Ascended Masters, other high dimensional beings of Light through 9th dimension and beyond. I connect to read current stream data and receive prophetic messages, channeled through drawing, painting, writing, singing, and even dancing. I access the consciousness of the universe, past lifetimes of skills, talents, abilities through "All Time" of past present future all existing now.

During my self discovery journey I found it interesting to learn through astrology that there is what is called a Pisces midheaven in my 9th house natal birth chart supporting my purpose of sharing this information from Cosmic Creation codes and records. I also have the ascended masters represented in my 12th house subconscious ready to speak to me, offering guidance and protection. Learning this and other information about myself through my awakening was fun, also serving as external confirmation when life is "interesting" enough to make one question their sanity due to the judgement, expectation, and limitations society projects from each person's beliefs and programs causing the illusion of separation. Pushing past that and staying committed to myself, I honor my truth and make no attempt to convince anyone of anything, merely sharing from a place of caring and love.

From a young age, as far back as I can remember I could see and feel energies/entities around me. This was both exciting with elementals, fairies, laws of the universe, angels and scary with shadow beings, demons being tricksters causing some detours along my journey. Even from elementary school I realized I was "different". I wasn't sure how to address this or even recognize fully how differently I processed and received information. I felt like the "adult" I am now, containing vast knowledge, however in a child's body, still maintaining the innocence and purity of that child yet sensing and feeling beyond my years. I would spend most my time outdoors—as I have always loved connecting with nature and animals. I recall stargazing, speaking to "home" "out there" and longing to return, to be someplace other than the Earth I knew; for it felt a cruel and hard place to understand, such a contrasting place from what I was most familiar with—Love. It took years of what I call "forgiving the forgetting" and remembering who I was and why I am here.

Along my journey many tools that assisted me, varying from self-help, astrology natal birth chart studying, becoming an Usui Reiki Master, completing five Theta-healing certifications, studying Human Design, taking various personality tests. It took hours of reflecting and going within to face and clear the lingering trauma and pain, healing years of suffering through anxiety, depression-suicidal thoughts, and abuse at physical, mental, emotional and spiritual levels. I felt called to explore, traveling many miles adventuring, unraveling the puzzle of my existence to "find", to "discover" my "self"... though it was when I stopped the seeking and searching, and stopped repeating patterns detrimental to myself, I realized I merely had to simply let go of all I had "known" for Light to enter and illuminate healing in those once dark aching spaces. I didn't need to be found, I wasn't lost, I needed to simply remember, remember who I am.

This doesn't mean I no longer feel contrasting moments of nerves, "challenges" or have "struggles", this means I create my bliss in those moments through acceptance, gratitude shifting my attitude and by no means I do not claim to know it all or have all the answers, I just know what *I do know* through life experience and remembrance of my Soul essence. I practice self-reflection, "shadow work" and continue to take ownership of my own actions. I hold integrity and honesty, honoring my boundaries, respecting self and others through pure intentions. I allow the hard work to be done and make life more fun even through the challenges!

Remember, self-love is not an hour or two of your day, self-love is not a treat or reward, self-love is being with yourself in each moment. Self-love is each breath you take, every step you make, and honoring along the way where YOUR light guides you. As we all anchor our Light brighter than ever before, like the "Lite-Brite" game, we are plugging into the grid creating our own picture, our own art of Life and shifting all reality. Self-love is the embodiment of YOUR life force energy. I do not allow others to persuade me or tell me what I should or shouldn't do from their point of view. I TRUST my SELF and keep choosing LOVE. I continue adventuring, expanding, remembering I am a Divine loved BEinG of Light. I will always be more than alright, and I believe the same is possible for you too.

Link to view Light Code transmissions & visions:

## About the Author

### SARAH ELKINS

My name is Sarah Elkins—NOW let me introduce my true self, the SOUL within this skin, LOVE's Light. My identity is not what you see, or words you read, grasping a fraction of my BEinG. I am not my age, sex or body. I am not my past, any of the tasks, or roles I've played. I am not my personality, or anything that has happened to me.

This life journey is just one story, one of many lifetimes; each intertwined, available to me now.

I am ONE—one spectral fragment of Divine, birthed from Source Mother/Father Love Consciousness; Universal Harmonic Vibrations, dancing into form as the Diamond Rainbow Rays bright flames of Truth, Purity, and Unity. I am here creating realms with Love's voice lifting the Veil. A Cosmic Mother Creatrix of this matrix. I come from Beyond the Stars, for healing, speaking and teaching for the Way of the Light. Some may say a Divine Conduit, High Priestess, or Ancient One; returned to share peace, bliss, and Love's message to assist in anchoring a new Higher Consciousness for the ascension of New Earth.

Allow me to guide you back to your true self, activating your Highest Divine Blueprint through SELF empowerment of your Soul Embodiment! "The journey begins within; where your Human meets your BEinG, finding the balance between."

If you feel INspired you may book with me for private or large events to begin your Genesis. I offer guest speaking, workshops/classes, meditations, healing sessions, attunements, Light code activations, Hathor Sound toning and more via phone, video, or in person. I look forward to connecting with you! You can find out more on my website or social media below:

Website: HumanMeetsBeing.com

Contact: 850610-1515 / Email HumanMeetsBeing@gmail.com

Social Media:
Facebook.com/IrisPriestess
Facebook.com/HumanMeets/Being
Instagram.com/human_meets_being/
Youtube.com/channel/UCiKi7p5u_5p28GYIu0NosCw  OR search  "Human Meets Being"
Podcast  https://anchor.fm/human-meets-being, Also available on itunes & Spotify

# EIGHT

## Penny Sisley

### FROM BROKEN TEEN TO SHAKTI

Mary was a stout, American born Philippine with short, salt and pepper hair. She had an engaging smile, beautiful, like a pearl necklace. I remember walking away from my family home for the last time, with her daughter, Sheri, who was adorned with crystal blue eyes, a wild blonde mane, and her Mama's smile. She came to help me gather my things. We were twelve.

My Mom had one condition upon marrying my Dad, and that was to move her as far away as possible from her family after he got out of prison. They ended up in Petaluma just west of the train tracks, on Petaluma Blvd. North, the old 101 freeway. Our house was on the divide of town. High-end farmland, Victorians and Craftsman style bungalows to the west, and miles of 60's floor plans to the east.

We lived right next door to Lasher Hatchery, a large brick building smelling of rotten eggs and musty cardboard; it hummed with incubators. My father worked there as a truck driver and came home each day for a scrambled egg breakfast.

Our home was a little white Craftsmen; it had a pink living room with painted blue floors, where three of the five siblings slept, one bathroom, two small bedrooms, a walk-through kitchen, and unfenced yards. Just to the left of the property was an endless golden field; I still remember holding my hands out to caress the tall "rabbit tail" grass and playing hide and seek with my siblings until dark.

By the time I was born, Dad was gone, except for weekly food money and occasional beach trips to Bodega Bay. By the time I was twelve, he was really gone.

I came home from school to a house full of packed boxes. My mom had no color in her face and looked lost in a house we could no longer call home. We had been evicted and were forced to go in different directions. I went to live with Mary and took a house cleaning job for $2.50 an hour.

Months went by as the old life with my family coiled into a shameful fireball and lived in the pit of my stomach. I missed the smell of warm tortillas and salty pinto beans. I craved familiarity.

Now I lived in a drafty, white Victorian house perched on top of the first steep hill on Oak Street, surrounded by what felt like the only known forest in Petaluma. Today I'd consider selling my firstborn for this architectural splendor with its barrel windows and towering ceilings. Still, to my young mind, it was empty and cold, and it's where I learned searing loneliness for the first time.

Ashamed of my situation, I exhausted myself with a fake smile and a cheerful attitude I forced myself to wear to avoid other peoples' questions—all happiness on the outside, the arctic winter on the inside. My constant incongruence blurred the line between lies and reality.

One time mom received some money and managed to keep us all together at Motel 6 for a week or two. My sisters and I had no idea why we were there or for how long. I can still see my mom sewing by hand at the edge of the bed while the rest of us made regular visits to the ice machine and watched the time tick by.

From then on, I saw my family on scattered holidays, which usually ended in pointless, entangled arguments. We were wounded.

I moved twenty-three times before the age of nineteen. Twice my dad came for me, once to live with him and his girlfriend. She came to one of my soccer games, a first for any adult in my life. Once she took me shopping because she noticed my shoes were worn out. I was amazed someone cared about my shoes.

The second time Dad came for me, I was fifteen. He rented a small house on Vallejo St. with my brother Frank who was twenty, also a truck driver, his girlfriend, and my mom. Dad made himself a room in the garage by hanging tarps from the ceiling into a rectangle. He had a bed, a light, and a shelf for his many books. He was trying again to be a Dad. I shared a room with mom.

Coming home late after school and work, I'd find her sitting in our room, sewing at the edge of the bed. I turned 16 that year, and like all of my other living situations, feelings went bad, Dad left, and I was back with Mary. She always let me come back until I could find another place to go. Her life was no amusement park; she was a hardworking housekeeper for the 'well to do,' a single mom trying to raise her own kids and pay the bills. Life was hard for all of us.

I worked three jobs to pay rent and to escape feeling my emotions. Fear, oddly enough, was not one of them. I remember taking the Golden Gate Transit bus to San Rafael on Fridays and Saturdays at midnight, so I could shuffle and sort newspapers until dawn. The road from the bus stop to work was a mile long and pitch black. Ink would barely be out of my lungs and hair before I returned again the following weekend.

Working helped me vacate a life that had become full of bad decisions, insecurity, and anger. My addiction to creating hurtful relationships haunted me. It was also the beginning of a long struggle as a workaholic.

One night at Mary's I was sitting on a white wicker sofa, deep in thought, trying to get warm, when she bounced in and handed me a beat up paperback book with a crazy looking old guy on the front cover who had a sinister smile. It was called "Your Erroneous

Zones" by Dr. Wayne Dyer. She said, "Here you go, Pen. I think you will really like this."

I looked through the book and began to devour the chapters one by one. I felt warmth releasing into my heart. At once, I knew his mind. At once, I was no longer alone.

From that moment on, I was home no matter where I lived. I now had a place in my mind I could call upon at any time to seek love, advice, and bits of harmony. I had never known this place before, not even on Petaluma Blvd. North.

What I didn't know is this man would raise me. He would teach me through his words for the next thirty-four years; how to come to know who I was and how I was a soul in a loving and giving Universe. And just like the Universe, he was always leaving the next most precious bread crumbs to seek.

I went on to open in ways I could never have imagined without the guidance of my dear teacher.

Dr. Dyer helped me understand the truth of who we really are – cosmic beings playing in a world of form, through a beloved and gifted human body. All because of love.

From there I journeyed to Italy and shook hands with the Pope. I went to Peru and climbed the tallest mountain. I hiked the Inca Trail and entered Machu Picchu from the 'Gate of the Sun'. My body was cleansed in mineral baths at the base of the Andes and healed by the earth. I explored the Galapagos Islands and became one with everything, even the king walrus who tried to pound me for looking his way…I loved him too. He was powerful!

I trusted myself enough to take chances and released much of the shame I buried in my teens. I forgave myself for the person I had become. My teacher not only taught me how to love but how to live. Most importantly, he gave me the strength to fight for happiness, and then in time, he taught me how to simply allow myself this wonderful birthright.

At twenty-eight I went to see him speak in San Francisco, and as I looked around the room, I witnessed fresh tears and wide-open smiles from a community pulsing with passion, truth, and inspiration. These were my people. It had been twelve years since I first held his book to my heart, and now, here I was! After the event, I stood in front of him for a book signing, thrilled to the height of my being, to which he paced out of his seat with open arms and said, "Hello Beautiful!" We embraced in a tight and endless hug as if he knew how far I had come.

What if all the suffering we go through is for a reason? Maybe there is a bigger picture, a plan or a direction where we all end up? Perhaps I was guided? I realized my life was not random; I was on a path.

The magical thing I found about this path is that life is always expanding—there's always more.

The things I went through during and after my childhood turned me into an intense workaholic and a killer light-seeking machine; I couldn't get enough. Hot and Cold. Light and Dark. Balanced and crazy. Always looking, searching, wanting. I crashed a few years ago when all I had done ended with me being a worn-out mom, buried in guilt for not Ever. Being. Enough.

Something was missing.

That's when I found my next teacher, Rajada.

Sitting in deep meditation in the middle of one hot afternoon, I heard a stern male voice say, "YOU ARE SHIVA!" I stood straight up as if lifted by the air itself. *Who the hell is Shiva?!*, I thought, miffed how having clairaudience still freaked me out.

Consulting Google, Wikipedia gave me the rundown and led me to Rajada's email.

"When the student is ready, the teacher will appear." Close enough.

I was guided to chakra work, energy centers, spinning discs. I had never really been into chakras, but here they were again.

Within eight weeks of working with my new teacher, revitalized with Eastern Philosophy, I realized how we gals love hanging out at the heart chakra and above. That's where I always wanted to spend my time—with the lightness of being. Decades spent. The challenge for many women is, we have a strong tendency to have poor function in our lower chakras, because of this desire to stay light. This unfortunately creates all the possible blocks and chaos anyone could ever want.

Ah Ha! Breakthrough!

The first three chakras, also referred to as the first sun, have to do with family, tribe, early childhood memories, karma, guilt, fear, doubt, desire, purpose, our physical self, relationships, sex, emotional cording, being grounded, boundaries, ego, self-worth, and our sheer will to create. This sun is all about being enough!

Having two boys of my own, I noticed immediately how in our culture we raise our boys to have strong lower chakras; our girls, not so much…

I learned all of us are a mixture of masculine and feminine energy, Shiva and Shakti. I could see the correlation between our world out of balance, and us—as the microcosms—out of balance. By raising the energy in the lower three chakras in females, we could open up a tremendous fortune of untapped intuition, solution and power within half of our society throughout our world.

Big Power. Big Changes. Big Possibilities.

Sounds exactly like the shift we need.

Yes, our world needs compassion, love, and caring, all of which is an honor to give, but giving it with the foundation of a sandcastle means we will not be heard, projects will not get built, money will not be raised, and ideas will not get the time to formulate. Everything takes a heck of a lot longer with a weaker first sun—sound familiar?

After working with my lower chakras, my business took off, my family healed from mental illnesses, our health went into alignment, and along with a deep sense of purpose, clarity and inspiration began to run my everyday life. Magic and synchronicity transformed everything. No more running from dawn till dusk in an attempt to prove I am enough. I was finally able to align with a belief I knew about but never understood; we are born worthy without having to do anything at all.

Let's get your first sun humming, so you can see for yourself, what life is like when your first three chakras are happy, productive, and balanced. Let's see where you go when you are not carrying around the past, with your brain in the future. Let's see if you can feel as light as a feather outside of meditation, right in the middle of a crowd or stressful situation.

That being said, have you ever spent the night at the bottom of the Grand Canyon? It's all happiness and amazement, pumping with warrior blood from the hike down. You wake up feeling accomplished and energized for the trek out. That is until you get to the rope bridge that crosses the Colorado River. Holy HellFire Damnation.

This journey is kind of like that, except your knees don't get weak, and you won't fall and die. And once you cross that bridge, you have made it to the other side!

I am teasing, and I'm not. Working with our first sun, the first three chakras, helps us release the shame of everything holding us back. Using Eastern techniques of mudras and mantra, the releasing happens at a cellular level. This will cause some emotional and possible physical discomfort, so make sure to drink lots of water, get your sleep, eat lots of fruits and vegetables and ease your schedule.

Make room in your life for change, and take care of yourself through this change. Remind yourself every day, I'm in charge, and I'm the one calling this stuff up to heal.

With the techniques I'm going to show you, stuff will come up. Unhealed heartbreaks will peak out again because your vessel will feel like a safer place to repair. You will remember details of memories you haven't thought about for years. Pay attention to what your body is showing you. When you feel ready, you will have an opportunity to process the feelings associated with the memories with the practice below. Then the memories will just be memories without the heavy anchors keeping us stagnate.

Understand one thing; it's going to be okay. You wouldn't be reading this far if you weren't ready for this monumental shift. You have been guided here for a reason. You are on a path. Wink.

## Tips to start your practice:

- Do this practice on an empty stomach when possible. This one trick is like a slingshot into your consciousness.

- Commit to 30 days. Review your ideas around commitment. Commitment is for you, it is not against you. It's to help your life hum at a level most only dream about. Yes, we can live at 60 percent and do okay in life, but if you want to live on the edge of your human body with full cosmic awareness, and enjoy living life in the 90 percent range, then make friends with commitment.

- Select a spot in your house where you will practice every day, either in the east or facing east. Make it beautiful and use your intention. You can make an altar or hang a pretty picture of a Goddess that resonates with you. Have a table with a space for your water and your journal in case you want to take some notes. Having a place and a set time helps others in the household to hold a space for you too.

- Choose a time that will win for you day after day. Morning is best because this practice sets up a beautiful day, but the very best time is when you can realistically make it work consistently.

.  .  .

THE FIRST CHAKRA is called the Muladhara, and it's located in Eastern Philosophy right at your anus. It represents the earth, is reddish in color, and loves the sound of drums. The energy here is represented by the **Goddess Ganesh**, a half boy, half elephant. Ganesh helps us to ground ourselves into the earth to keep us stable.

The sound we make to heal the first chakra is LAM, which is called a beej mantra.

We place our hands under our rear, rotate our upper body in a circle going to the right, saying LAM, while imagining the earth beneath us, the molten lava and rocks crushing together. We also imagine Ganesh stomping those rocks while listening to amazing drum beats from your favorite YouTube or Spotify list. Do this for a few minutes while clenching your anus and internally lifting it up and down if you are a gal, or swing it slightly forward if you are male. Increase the time as you get better.

Start with three minutes per chakra and increase the time to five minutes per chakra in one week.

THE SECOND CHAKRA is called the Swadhistana, and it's located in Eastern Philosophy at your linga (penis) or your clitoris. It represents water, is orange in color, and loves the sound of a creek or waterfall. The energy here is represented by the **Goddess Kali**; a fully armored female warrior who is sticking out her red tongue. She is fighting for you!

The sound we make to balance the second chakra is VAM

Place the Yoni Mudra (see below illustration for hand formation) at the second chakra (clitoris/penis), rocking our upper body forward and back gently while chanting VAM. Imagine snakes wiggling through water while listening to a water track for more power.

YOGA

Yoni mudra

THE THIRD CHAKRA is called the Manipura, and it's located in Eastern Philosophy at your navel. It represents the element of fire and is yellow. The energy here is represented by the **Goddess Durga**, who we often see riding a lion. She is a veera, a fierce warrior Goddess who supports you in burning your doubt, fear, and the chattering mind.

The sound we make to heal the third chakra is

RAM.

Place the Shiva Linga Mudra (see below illustration for hand formation), with the left hand placed just beneath the navel. Take three rapid breaths in through the mouth, and breath out once through the nose. Continue this breath at a good pace ten times while imagining a huge bonfire in your navel. As you continue this breath and mudra, imagine yourself throwing in all of your doubt, fear, and mindless chatter into the fire. Throw in uncomfortable situations, guilt, regrets, and anything that intuitively comes up. Do it as many times as you feel necessary. Some days it will take longer than others. Once you feel complete, chant **RAM** nine times, dropping your chin. Feeling hot is normal in this exercise.

## YOGA

Shiva Linga mudra
Energy changing mudra

FINISH your practice with this **AKSHAR MALA** (Sanskrit words sewn together) mantra while moving your hands up and down the body:

aeem (sounds like "I'm") (place hand over mouth, not touching)

kleem (place two hands over heart)

sauh (sounds like "so huh") (place both hands on your yoni or linga)

sauh (again) (keep both hands on your yoni or linga)

kleem (place two hands on your heart)

aeem (place hand over mouth, not touching)

This powerful mantra represents three energies within us: the throat chakra, the heart chakra, and the second chakra. Saying this mantra is helping us integrate the practice into our physical body, marrying it with our energetic body.

Do this very particular practice for 30 days. After some initial discomfort while you burn away heaviness,  you will begin to feel a calm come over your heart, and a heightened sense of clarity, while your next most important steps to true happiness and success begin to emerge through your powered-up first sun. This is just the beginning. Namaha.

## About the Author

### PENNY SISLEY

Penny Sisley is a Certified Life Coach, a Mentor and a Mystic. As the founder of Advanced Life Mastery, she offers women's groups, chant circles, group coaching, and international mentorships.

Utilizing EFT/Tapping, Chakra Science, Mantras, Mudras and the Mystic arts of Shakti Wisdom, Penny guides women to clear their energy bodies, shedding layers of cultural and DNA dysfunction. With increased equanimity, her clients awaken to the Divine Observer within; seeker becomes Source, and a foundational shift occurs. From this new and revitalized vantage point, life becomes an inspiring and expansive journey, where true heart action and bliss can spring.

Penny is also an Executive Producer for the upcoming film, "America's First Guru," a project very dear to her heart. When she's not spending time with her family, or leading inspired groups for Gals, you can find her dancing under the moonlight, singing mantras, or reading in the backyard with her doggie, Sydney.

Website:
https://www.advancedlifemastery.com/
psisley@sbcglobal.net
Facebook:
https://www.
facebook.com/AdvancedLifeMasteryPennySisleyCoach

Instagram:
https://www.instagram.com/pennysisley/?hl=en
LinkedIn:
https://www.linkedin.com/in/penny-sisley/

# NINE

## Fiona Tate

### WEAVING OURSELVES BACK TOGETHER - AWAKENING THE LIGHT WITHIN.

I am a holistic counsellor, psychotherapist, and healer. I have spent over 25 years studying mind/body psychology, consciousness, metaphysics, and healing. In my practice, I work with energies beyond the veil and embodied presence to facilitate higher states of consciousness in my clients that facilitate deep healing. When we are in this Soul alignment, we are the creators and are in harmony. This chapter is about accessing higher states of consciousness and soul alignment through psychotherapy.

There is a tapestry of Light that weaves through every one of our cells, every sinew, every fibre of our bodies, and connects us all. We live within a vibrational field of energy; the entire human journey is within the quantum field; it is all energy. We are connected to a higher power, a magical force far greater than us; call it God, Great Spirit, The Universe. This is the flow of consciousness. Our soul is part of the universal consciousness and inhabits the body for our lifetime. Full embodied presence allows consciousness to flow freely through us, connecting to this tapestry of Light. This is the free flow of spirit through our body, mind, and energy field. Our energetic frequency communicates, and our Soul harmonises with the Universe.

I had this flow of consciousness in my body and spirit interrupted when I was a child.

When I was nine, I suffered a massive head injury from a horse-riding accident. My skull was fractured, my brain was bleeding, and I was in a coma for five weeks. It was an acquired brain injury that the doctors thought I might never recover from. They weren't even sure if I would ever wake up or if I did if I would be able to live a normal life. When I did wake up, my whole right side was paralysed, and I couldn't talk. I had to relearn everything. It was a slow process! Doctors advised my parents not to send me to school because it would be a waste of money, but here I am; with many years of study and experience under my belt.

Soon after waking up from my coma, my dad taught me to meditate. I believe it was meditation that helped save my life, weaving my brain back together and weaving new neural pathways. I remember my dad saying he wondered if I would grow up to be psychic because many people who have severe head injuries as children do. Now that I've studied neurophysiology, I understand why that is the case. My cortex (which is the thinking/logical part of the brain) was shut down, whereas my amygdala (the subconscious/ spiritual/ intuitive brain) was amplified. This allows the cortex more communication with the amygdala, which I will explain later, is crucial for spiritual awakening. Deeper access to the amygdala allows for heightened intuitive awareness. Scientific evidence suggests that the altered state of consciousness created by the shock and trauma of a head injury heightens perception, ESP (extra-sensory perception), and psychic awareness.

Years later, I was able to recall the near-death experience I had at the moment of the accident. Everything went black. There was no light in my body, no light in my consciousness. Then a tiny pinhole of light pierced the darkness. I moved toward the light, and an angel stood with me. The light grew bigger and began to fill my body. It felt healing and like I was filling with a newly awakened consciousness. Near-death experiences have been found to alter the electromagnetic field in and around the brain. This alteration produces a type of "micro-seizure" that makes people sensitive to the perception of alternate realities and altered states of consciousness.

It has been my life's journey to heal and process the trauma and shock of this accident and to ground and inhabit my body fully with that light. I also have always had heightened awareness, psychic abilities, and heightened sensitivity to see and feel beyond the veil. This is my soul calling—to help others become more embodied and to connect with this light.

I have spent over two decades studying psychology, metaphysics, mind/body healing and meditation, to understand the ways that consciousness flows. I have studied different philosophical understandings of how this consciousness gets interrupted and how we can heal it, to facilitate realignment and higher states of consciousness.

I am an empath and have been psychic since a child. In this chapter, I share my journey of understanding how we live within a larger field of energy, how we access realms beyond the veil, and how that strengthens and informs my psychotherapy practice.

I've come to see how our mind and our ego state make us forget our inherent connection with pure consciousness. Over time, thoughts and emotions get woven through the tapestry and create distortions in our energy bodies. Deep subconscious conditioning and trauma interrupt and block the flow of consciousness through our cells, mind, energy field, and chakras. As we grow up, the magic is taken from us as we lose our connection. We live in a thinking rational world, so we lose connection to our spiritual wisdom and intuition. This is the splitting of the two parts of the brain. The cortex and amygdala cease to communicate and become mutually exclusive. We get conditioned and programmed, and we lose connection to source. We forget who we are. The purpose of healing, our soul mission, is to access higher states of consciousness. We need to bring consciousness back into every cell, every fibre, to allow consciousness to flow evenly through the body. The body, mind, and spiritual energies are intricately woven together, and we anchor light through our bodies. You can say, then, that healing is a remembering of who we are, a process of reconnection. Our healing journey is about raising our frequency, raising our consciousness, connecting to our soul, and remembering who we are.

When I was eighteen, I started reading tarot. Tarot is a psychic development tool used to access subtle energies and tune into higher frequencies beyond the veil. I use it to tap into the subconscious and for quantum healing. Through the symbolism of the images, the cards can access the deeper layers of the mind. Before each reading, I use a pendulum to assess which chakras in my client are blocked.

Tarot readings access subconscious blocks and brings them to conscious awareness. After readings, the chakras are always cleared. This is magical and seemed supernatural, but after studying neurophysiology in my Master's degree, I now understand energetically how this is possible. The symbolism of the cards taps into the deeper parts of the brain in the limbic system, the amygdala. This part of the brain is connected to the subconscious and deep emotional processing. It also connects to the body, nervous system, and energy field. Tarot helps to expand awareness, to lift beyond ordinary consciousness, bringing communication and remembering between these two parts of the brain.

The amygdala is inaccessible when we are in our logical thinking brain (cortex). The amygdala is connected to our subconscious, body, and spiritual self. The cortex and the amygdala are mutually exclusive. When affected by trauma, the circuit between the cortex and amygdala is affected, and they don't communicate properly.

When I was learning tarot and psychic work, I lived in Nimbin in regional New South Wales, Australia. I had a mentor, Brian, and we did a lot of meditation and psychic development. One day I saw a beautiful egg-shaped crystal in my meditation. I asked Brian what type of crystal it was, feeling certain it was important for me to get one. "It's a fluorite. We can get one tomorrow in Nimbin", he said. I told him, "No, my crystal is in Byron Bay crystal shop." He replied,

"Oh, we can get it next week then." The weekend came, and a very strange series of events landed me at a musical gathering, doing tarot readings by donation. One guy apologised that he had nothing to offer and sat down. After the reading, he was blown away by the accuracy, so he reached into his pocket and placed something in the palm of my hand, and closed my fist around it. He went inside to dance. Inside my palm was the exact egg-shaped fluorite crystal I had seen in my meditation! I went inside to tell him, and he said he had bought the crystal only a few hours ago from the shop in Byron Bay. This was amazing, a truly magical moment! This was a reflection to me of my vibration being aligned and in the flow of the Universe.

The other day I was teaching my daughter to ride my horse. I told her to keep her body strong but calm because the horse can sense fear. I explained that if she is afraid, he will sense it and get anxious. They are communicating through their nervous system. I thought about this later. This is attunement. In relationships, we communicate with our nervous system. Our nervous systems can co-regulate or can dysregulate together (this is a lot of my work when working with couples). We communicate through a very subtle frequency of consciousness that we hold, through our nervous system and vibrational frequency. This is the way our energy body communicates with the universe. Just as the horse is attuned to my daughter, the universe is attuned to you. The universe responds to your energetic frequency.

I always knew I was a healer and wanted to work in this field. After high school, I completed a Psychology degree at university, but psychology was too cerebral and didn't seem holistic enough. I wanted to work with the spiritual, transpersonal aspects of self. I continued with studies of tarot and energy healing and studied the mind/body connection and quantum healing. I then studied Shiatsu therapy, which works on the meridian system to corrects the flow of energy (consciousness) in the body. I felt I was getting closer… I studied and practiced vipassana meditation and Buddhist psychology, and over the years, attended many ten-day silent retreats. I continued reading tarot and doing quantum healing and working with deep subconscious patterns, and also studied transpersonal art therapy, followed by studying Counselling and Psychotherapy.

My psychotherapy studies simply consolidated everything else I have ever studied and completed the puzzle. Psychotherapy is a psycho-spiritual approach to healing that addresses the deepest levels of self and offers a space where I can integrate the different theories, approaches, and interventions I know about working with the deepest layers of the mind that incorporate the spiritual aspects of self.

## We Are Influenced by Subtle Energy

We are very intricate beings, influenced on a very deep level by energy, subconscious patterns, neural pathways that have formed or been lost, electrical impulses, and consciousness (Spirit). We are influenced and affected by the energy within us as well as the energy surrounding us. When we surrender, we become more embodied and in alignment with flow. When we are in alignment, and we raise our vibrational frequency, and we are Divine Creators. Spirit breathes through us, and the light breathes through our bodies.

I remember a time, standing on the side of the highway with my thumb out, my heavy backpack on, when I was in the French part of Switzerland. I was hitching from Germany back to Italy and was at a fork in the road. I needed to go straight ahead, but everyone who passed either didn't speak English or was turning off. It was getting late, and it felt like it was going to rain. Fear crept in, I got scared, and my energy contracted. What if I didn't get a ride? What if I was left here? I felt lost and alone. I looked around and saw a big tree I could sleep under for the night if needed. Then I suddenly realised that if someone showed me a map, I would have absolutely no idea where I was! In this moment, I experienced an incredible sense of freedom and expansion, and it shifted my energy. I was not lost. I belonged to the Earth. So I prayed, I asked the Universe for support. I kid you not, at that exact moment, a young couple pulled up and offered to drive me to where I needed to go!

I travelled for a couple of years, learning the language of the universe and developing my intuition. The universe has her own language and frequency, and if we tune into our intuition and our heart, we can be guided. We communicate with the universe, similar to the attunement of my daughter and the horse. I travelled with my journal and wrote every day, listening to the signs, synchronicities, and waves of magic, staying in alignment, and co-creating my journeys.

When we are in flow, we create our reality. We are multidimensional beings, much larger and more powerful than we understand. There is only a small portion of our consciousness in this 3D realm, which means that there are aspects of our consciousness which is not in this realm. This gives the opportunity for us to expand our consciousness and connect with other dimensions. Our soul extends beyond our physical body into our auric field, our higher self, and universal consciousness. We are also connected to higher dimensional beings who are with us. There are different layers to our energy body and to our auric field, and we are connected to source and the angelic realms. Our soul already knows. We just need to reconnect and remember.

Humanity as a collective is moving into higher vibrational frequencies. When we are healing and growing, we are raising our frequency and vibration. Love, unity, peace, and higher states of awareness are all higher vibrational states. Energies like fear, anger, separation, and judgement are lower states of vibration.

Healing has to take place on all levels and needs to be as multidimensional as we are—it needs to address all aspects of ourselves. I've found that counselling can address surface level problems, whereas Psychotherapy looks beneath the surface to the underlying causes of problems. The deep work of psychotherapy addresses unresolved childhood trauma, energy distortions, and patterns that have developed over time. Psychotherapy is a deep operation of the mind, and spiritual psychotherapy takes into account the energies and spiritual forces beyond the veil that are also influencing and impacting the process. Psychotherapy is a very intricate art form. It's an intuitive process that has taken many years of experience, intuitive development, and personal practice to refine, and I will be forever learning. I absolutely love this work. I love combining a very unique set of tools and approaches to help my clients.

I understand psychotherapy and healing to be a sacred process of weaving those disconnected parts of the brain back together, weaving our spirits back into the fabric of our body, and weaving the light back into our cells. We do this by entering the body, surrendering, and deepening. Embodiment requires vulnerability, softness, and surrender. Our body then becomes a portal for higher consciousness, a portal of light, a vessel of love.

However, it's not all love and light; spiritual growth means expanding our consciousness in every direction, up and down, dark and light, inwards and outwards. Through this work, we expand our capacity. We need to face our inner darkness and shadows and reach up to the heavens to the light of the angelic realms. As we work inward, we also expand upward. So, the spiritual journey will always ask you to go to your depths, explore the shadows—peeling back the layers to become more deeply embodied and connected.

Many of my clients are on the spiritual path. The deeper we go on our spiritual path, the deeper we go into ourselves. As we raise our frequency to the light, we need to *embody* the light. Embodying a higher consciousness will awaken the deepest traumas where the light cannot get in. This is the work. So we lean in.

Rudolf Steiner was a great philosopher and spiritual teacher. He was the founder of anthroposophy, which is a path of knowledge to guide the Spiritual in the human being to the Spiritual in the Universe. In Steiner philosophy, it is said that the soul takes seven years to incarnate. In other schools of thought, it is said that most of our subconscious programming happens in the first seven years of life. So, the subconscious is formed as we are incarnating! I believe that inhibiting subconscious patterns are from when the soul was not properly incarnated because of a trauma or emotion that was experienced that wasn't able to be integrated.

The first seven years are very formative and can have a huge impact on our subconscious patterns, beliefs, and our embodiment. Events that are too overwhelming to be processed at the time are hidden from conscious awareness, accumulating in the subconscious.

When emotions that are not processed get stuck in the body in those early years, the incarnation process is inhibited. So we arrive at adulthood only an echo of our pure essence, our pure self. Fragments of our Soul are left behind. Also, along the journey, aspects of ourselves get denied, or shamed, or disowned. In psychotherapy, inner child healing or inner child rescue is Soul retrieval work, integrating our lost selves back together.

If a child grows up in a family where she has to tip-toe around a parent, doesn't get emotional needs met, has to accommodate for a parents dysfunction, or is invalidated, there is attachment trauma, the child's energy body will be distorted, and there is most likely internalised shame. These energy distortions manifest in a number of ways in adulthood, for example—anxiety, relationship problems, or substance abuse. To fix these, we need to work with the cognitive distortions as well as the energy body. Additionally, strong emotional and energetic ties from the past can be long-lasting, which may inhibit us in later years. In psychotherapy, these energetic ties and chords can be healed to help us to be more autonomous, empowered, and sovereign.

## Our Healing Journey

Beginning the path of healing can be overwhelming to think about. We have all accumulated so much pain or trauma that was not integrated or processed properly. We then develop coping strategies and defence mechanisms to get through each day, or we numb by drinking or overworking to avoid ourselves, or we end up in toxic or co-dependent relationships. These are all extremely deep patterns that are held in the nervous system and energy body. Life is full, with so many demands. How to cope? How to do the work? Jeez, it took forty years for all this baggage to accumulate. It's going to take years to process it all! It's too much.

The good news is that it's not going to take that long. The past lives in us, in this moment. Every experience you've ever had, and every unprocessed emotion, is catalogued in your nervous system. Your nervous system and energy body are like a doorway, a portal into the real you. You are still there. Your Soul is calling you home.

We are all like Babushka dolls, with our younger selves living inside of us. Those younger selves create energy templates that echo through our timeline until healed. If there is a little four-year-old inside of you that feels abandoned or unloved, she is still there—sitting, waiting to be loved and validated. The effects of childhood wounds ripple through your nervous system, through your vibrational energy field and can have a devastating impact on your relationships, self-esteem, and mental health. However, this trauma can also be an access point, leading you into deep healing and home to yourself, to your Soul.

Our journey begins with self-awareness and self-enquiry. We begin to question our patterns or behaviours and look deeper into some dynamics in our family or situations in childhood. Or we may not. It may take some big event like a relationship breakup or mental health breakdown to take us on a deeper journey of enquiry.

Healing can be challenging. The process of tending to what lies underneath can be scary. The journey of moving in, unravelling the knots, and tending to the threads takes time. Neural pathways have been diverted, shame has kept us from moving in, subconscious belief systems have become forged into our psyche, and boundaries have been violated and distorted. The process of healing is one that needs to be integrated, slowly, delicately, and sacredly, to a feeling of being safe inside our body. As we work with the different parts of the brain and weave ourselves back together, our capacity builds, our nervous system becomes more regulated, and our world becomes more manageable.

I see clients with a range of symptoms; feeling disconnected, low self-esteem, patterns of self-sabotage, challenging relationships, anxiety, depression, history of trauma, not feeling good enough, spiritual crisis or transition—the list goes on. Some clients come to me feeling completely broken and like there's something wrong with them. I tell them, "There is nothing wrong with you. This is a normal and healthy reaction to what you have experienced." What has happened over time, and why these defences have built up, is an intricate tapestry of energy, spirit, emotions, cognitions, and patterns that have been woven together.

We cannot fast-track healing through a short course. Quick fixes can potentially do more harm than good and be re-traumatising. We cannot charge through our defence mechanisms—they are protection. Your nervous system is protecting you. To stop you from being crippled by fear or trauma, defences build up to protect you from the pain, so you can continue to function. Defence mechanisms keep us feeling safe. Healing and moving through these patterns is sacred work that needs to be respected and navigated gently.

Once we understand the function of defences and how we got to be this way, the work has begun. I help educate my clients about what has happened and why this has happened, energetically and cognitively, and then how we can easily move through and heal this together.

The purpose is not an end point that we need to rush towards. The purpose is the journey of re-establishing a sense of safety in the body, slowly erode old defences, develop a new sense of awareness, invite in a new way of being, meet our bodies in a new way, and expand our consciousness to higher states of being. Reading books and doing the work on your own can only get you so far because our brain is the only organ in our body that cannot regulate on its own. We need to be in the presence of a trained therapist, and our nervous system needs to be coregulated by the presence of a grounded, fully embodied practitioner.

On a higher level, humanity and the planet is going through a process of ascension and awakening into higher consciousness and higher frequencies. As a collective, we are healing years of oppression, shame, fear, trauma, and suffering. As we rise to higher frequencies of light, the darker fears and pain will surface. As healers and lightworkers, we all need to choose our consciousness at this time. These are big times for all of us. Raising our vibration, raising our frequency, and not getting drawn into the collective fear will help the collective consciousness of humanity.

I invite you to let this book awaken a new sense of awareness within you, for you to explore and deepen your own healing journey. It is a sacred, intimate journey of gently coming home to your body and reconnecting with your Soul.

Go gently. This is sacred work. Welcome home.

## About the Author

FIONA TATE

Fiona is a registered psychotherapist, healer, and meditation teacher, based in the Yarra Valley, Victoria, Australia. She has previously published a childrens meditation book *The Magic Tree, and other meditations to Help Children Sleep.*

Drawing on her experience from over 20 years studying and practicing mind/body therapy, intuition, consciousness, psychology and psychotherapy, she uses an integrated approach, drawing on evidence based clinical interventions, and intuitive energy medicine, traditional wisdom and spiritual practices. Fiona aims to empower her clients, resolving conflicts and trauma, inner child healing, and through the lens of embodiment, helping to regulate her clients nervous system.

In her chapter *Weaving ourselves back together, Awakening the Light Within*, Fiona explains her awakening journey, beginning from a young child when she had and a near death experience.

We all have an inner light, and the spiritual journey is to awaken it. Psychotherapy is a gentle art, weaving back together the parts of ourselves that have been fragmented along the way. Fiona draws upon a wealth of experience and wisdom to explain the essence of the spiritual journey and her psychotherapy practice.

Fiona has a BSc (psychology), Graduate Diploma Counselling and completed all coursework for her Masters in Psychotherapy.

Website: FionaTate.com.au

Facebook: Fiona Tate - Holistic Psychotherapist & Healer

Instagram:  fiona_tate_meditation

TEN

# Becky Payne

## MOTHERHOOD: A SPIRITUAL AWAKENING

I often hear mothers say once they have children, they lose themselves. For me, it was the opposite. When I birthed my baby, I found myself. I believe I was able to achieve that because I had a solid understanding of myself already. I have attended countless trainings, retreats and read so many books on spirituality, self-healing, self-help, yoga, and meditation. You name it, I've tried. I had worked on myself so deeply that I eventually had to share these teachings with others. When I had my baby, I had already had my first spiritual awakening.

Let's start at the beginning—the beginning of my first spiritual awakening. When I had my first awakening, I began to see the world in a different light. I started to become aware of my own energy and the energy around me. I had a strong desire to move in the direction of that awareness and make positive and sometimes hard changes to better my life. There is no one way that a person can experience an awakening. Each person will awaken in their own time when they are ready. I hope my story helps you to find the path that leads to your spiritual awakening.

Growing up, I didn't know anything about energy work, clairvoyance, healing, or spirituality. But I did know that I felt everything. I knew that when we went to church, I felt the depth of each and every person in that room. I deeply felt every funeral, wedding, and christening that had taken place. My eyes would fill with tears, my heart would race, and my stomach would fill with butterflies that would later whisper to my soul. I knew that I had these feelings and that they would bubble up when I was around other people. I could be with one person or surrounded in a crowd, but I was connected to each person I was with. If I went to a concert or a sporting event, it could sometimes be overwhelming, all that energy floating around for me to absorb. I didn't yet have the tools to protect myself from everyone else's energy. I didn't understand these feelings. Why was I depressed? Why was I anxious? Unsure of what I was feeling, I buried these overwhelming emotions. I hid them deep below the surface, where I eventually drowned them in alcohol, antidepressants, and anti-anxiety medications. I would have to crawl out of that hole eventually. At that time, that was the only way I knew how to deal with what I was feeling and taking in every day.

Later, I would discover that I was actually feeling everyone else's emotions and taking them on as my own. Welcome to the life of an everyday empath. We are everywhere. If you are reading this, I am willing to bet that you have already tapped into your psychic abilities or are on the verge of a spiritual awakening too. Trust me, you will find peace through all the noise and palpable energy. Start with awareness and keep moving forward.

My first introduction into the wellness world was when I became a massage therapist. I was in an unhealthy marriage and craving something that would fill the voids that were seemingly everywhere I turned. I absolutely loved it. There was something so soothing about touch, and I started to notice people's energy in a different way which also made me more aware of my own. This was the very beginning of my self-healing journey. It would still take me years to get to my initial "awakening".

As I continued my work as a massage therapist, my mind began to slow down and then eventually started to open. I was introduced to reiki. A totally new way of seeing the world! Reiki is an ancient healing practice based on the belief that we all have a life force energy moving through our bodies. Reiki helps to balance that energy. With my first reiki attunement or initiation, I had a revelation and a deep spiritual awakening. This attunement changed my life forever. Shortly after my first initiation into reiki, the finger where my wedding ring still lived broke out into a rash, and tears endlessly streamed down my face. If that wasn't a sign to get out, I don't know what else could have told me so boldly to move on. I eventually listened, got divorced, and met the love of my life, who is still beside me today. Believe it or not he was and still is my support through all the steps of this and my next spiritual awakening. I practiced reiki, received my second degree attunement and after that, I became a reiki master/teacher, a yoga teacher, an aesthetician, and a meditation guide. I had done so much work on myself and now it was time to help others heal. I was on a mission to show people that we can heal ourselves through awareness. I later named myself a holistic healing guide in hopes that that title would encompass all I offer. Then one day, after we sent my partners grown kids off into the world, surprise, we are pregnant!! What? I am 39 and have lots to do, I don't have time for a baby? It is an understatement to say that I was wrong and on the verge of my second and most profound spiritual awakening.

When I look back at the series of events that led to my baby's soul merging with my own, it all makes sense. The universe literally laid out the path and set the foundation for my baby to safely enter the world. It's quite amazing really. The more we allow ourselves to flow with the universe's plan, the more easily our time in this life goes. When we are open to receive what we are meant to, and ready to let go of what we are not meant to have or be, an endless stream of miracles awaits. My little miracle had been waiting for me for a long time.

I would be lying if I said I didn't want to have a baby or didn't know that one day I would. I am a clairvoyant after all, I knew it, even if I didn't want to admit it. Clairvoyance is the ability to gain information about an object, person, location, or physical event through extrasensory perception. I am not special by any means, I truly believe we all encompass psychic "gifts", we just have to be made aware of them. Every psychic I've ever seen told me I would have a baby. They all said, my baby was waiting for me. My baby waited until I was in the best physical, mental, and spiritual shape of my life before she arrived. When those three aligned, she made her way to me. I was the happiest I had ever been when she made her cozy home in my womb. My Lucy, my light, settled in just fine as I adjusted to the idea that I was going to have a baby! She is truly the most amazing gift I have ever been given. Lucy is my greatest teacher. She began teaching me from the moment I knew of her existence. This is where my true spiritual awakening began.

I can't be sure that what I am about to say happens to everyone but, I have a feeling that it does. It was true for me. My chakras were greatly affected by the life growing inside of me. Chakras are energy centers in our body. They each hold a specific energy and are often referred to as wheels of light.

If you aren't familiar with the chakras or energy centers in the body here is a simple explanation of what energy each chakra represents:

**The Root Chakra** is located at the base of the spine and represents the energies of safety, security, and feeling grounded.

**The Sacral Chakra** is located just below your belly button and holds the energies of sensuality, sexuality, creativity, and passion.

**The Solar Plexus Chakra** is located just above the belly button and holds your personal power, confidence, and boundaries.

**The Heart Chakra** is located at your heart center and governs our ability to have love and compassion for yourself and others.

**The Throat Chakra** is located at your throat and is your center of communication and living your highest truth.

**The Third Eye Chakra** is located at your forehead and is your center of intuition and inner wisdom.

**The Crown Chakra** is located at the top of your head and is your energetic center or spirituality and your connection to all.

When I was pregnant my crown chakra closed. I went inward to nourish and grow my baby. I dove deeper inside myself then I knew was possible. My root chakra closed completely—I needed a safe place for my daughter to grow so I instinctively closed my root chakra. I was beginning to create a nourishing circle of energy for her to thrive in. My body, as all pregnant bodies do, physically closed itself to outside energy through my mucus plug. Nothing that wasn't supposed to get to my baby was going to get in. I had a force-field of energy protecting her from myself and all my spirit guides. Spirit Guides are entities that remain as a disembodied spirit to act as a guide or protector to a living person. My body was filled with energy from myself and my growing baby and that's all. I was closed off to outside influences and my only job was to allow my baby to grow in the healthiest environment I could provide for her. For nine months I had a circle of energy moving back and forth from my body to my baby's. No energy left. Energy constantly and consistently building and building until one night my water broke. A literal and metaphorical release of life and the purest energy you can imagine! Wow! What a rush! I won't bore you with the details of the birth, but, 44 hours later my sweet Lucy came out of my body and was placed on my chest. If you have never experienced this—it is surreal, certainly spiritual, and the most intense and beautiful moment of my life! Bliss, tears, laughter, and so much love as I held her in my arms for the very first time. I'll never forget that moment. The energy release of birth is strong, immense, and so fucking powerful! It's not just the physical body that changes in pregnancy and on the journey to motherhood. The energetic body also takes on a new dimension. If I haven't already convinced you that motherhood is a spiritual awakening, keep reading.

The day my daughter was born, so was I. My baby is, to this day, my greatest teacher.

As we began our new life together all the lessons that I thought I had learned were reintroduced and retaught to me. She has taught me many things and reminded me of some lessons I have already learned. I thought I was "good" at being in the present moment. I've built so many yoga classes and written countless meditations around that theme... wasn't I an "expert" at this by now? Sure I was aware of it, but my Lucy has shown me what it truly means to be present. My root chakra was finally balanced. I was grounded and connected to the Earth and to the basic needs of life. When she needed to be fed, everything stopped. I stopped, no matter where I was or what I was doing, I breastfed my baby. We were both in that moment and only that moment, nothing else mattered. We were focused and present. When she was tired, once again, we both paused. It didn't matter what I had planned to do, everything came to a halt, and I soothed my sweet girl until she drifted off. We were in that moment and only that moment. We breathed together. We paused. Nothing else matters but that moment in time. My root chakra was completely balanced. She will continue to teach me this as we stumble through life together. This is not a lesson that can be taught in one session, it is a skill that takes many years to "master". Lucy and I have so much time to work on being present together.

After Lucy showed me how to be truly in the moment, she then asked me energetically, to teach her everything I know. I began to love myself more. After all, I had just grown a human in my body, birthed, and fed her with milk from my breasts. How could I not love and honor my body more than ever? My Heart chakra was now full of more love and compassion for myself and others that I even knew to be possible. By showing her how to love and care for herself, I began to love and care for myself even more. My Heart Chakra was activated and balanced.

As I continued to awaken, my third eye chakra was stimulated. I have never trusted my intuition as much as I do now. No matter how many times I had taught others how to listen to their inner guide, I was really hearing her for the first time. She was clear and told me everything that I needed to know. I don't doubt myself anymore. If something doesn't feel right, I don't waste my energy on it. If something needs to change or I need to let something go—it's gone. No regrets. I trust myself. I do what is best for myself and family now, and I don't feel bad about it. I am grateful for my intuition. My Third eye chakra is balanced and ready to go!

After her birth, my solar plexus shines more brightly than ever before. I truly stand in my power now. I am more confident than I ever thought I could be. I create solid boundaries in my work and in my personal life. I no longer feel guilty for it. It actually makes me feel good! In my mind I'm like, "Go Becky! You did it again, doesn't that feel good?!" And it feels so good! An extra added benefit to creating more solid boundaries and standing in my power is that it has actually inspired others around me to do the same. My Solar Plexus chakra is balanced and glowing boldly.

As my solar plexus chakra continued to awaken, I also noticed my throat chakra opening. Pre-baby, I had a hard time communicating what I needed or what I really wanted to say. After the baby, I speak my truth with much more ease and grace. After all, I don't have time for miscommunication, I have lots of wonderful things to do! It isn't always easy to communicate what needs to be said, but it is necessary for living the best life you can.

My crown chakra was a little slower to open in the sense that I didn't want to let everyone in all at once. I wanted to keep an energetic container around our family, and let's face it, having a baby in a pandemic helped me do that too. As my crown chakra opened, I felt a calling to teach Lucy different aspects of spirituality. I wanted to teach Lucy Reiki and I did. I have never taught children before, so I let intuition be my guide. I simply talked about reiki and showed her reiki. I had been giving her reiki since the day I was made aware of her existence. She has been practicing reiki since she was one! The first time she laid her hands on me with intention my world opened-up even more. I was in awe of her gentle, healing energy.

I searched for books for her on spirituality, meditation, reiki, and other wellness ways of life. The messages I wanted for her weren't out there, so I wrote my own. Talk about sacral chakra opening! I have always loved writing but have never done anything with my creations. I believe that when I birthed Lucy, my sacral chakra was cracked wide open and all that creative and passionate energy came spilling out with her body. That energy had been building for nine months and now it had been set free! This has led me to write an entire series of books called Little Healers. What!? I am a writer? It is almost like a living dream. She has awakened me to my true potential. I am living a different way now, I see life in a new way, in a new light. Life is clear and bright now. Spiritual awakening? Yeah —I would say so!

This is just the start. Lucy has created this space for me to awaken even more and you can bet on it—I am going to take her up on her offerings. We have an energy agreement beyond this life. We will move energy back and forth for the rest of our time together in this life and beyond. We have so much to learn from each other. Birthing my child and becoming a mother is my most important accomplishment yet and my true spiritual awakening. I can't wait to watch us come alive even more and bathe in the beauty of our energetic, psychic, and spiritual gifts as our lives unfold together. I am inspired and awake and ready to learn and grow, to become what I was meant to be on this Earth. Motherhood is a spiritual awakening.

## About the Author

BECKY PAYNE

Becky Payne is a holistic healing guide and the owner of Becky's Skincare and Bodywork, a healing studio in South Portland, Maine. In addition to being a self-published author, she is a Reiki Master/Teacher, Yoga Teacher, Massage Therapist, Aesthetician, Meditation Guide and holds a bachelor's degree in Social and Behavioral Science with a minor in Women's Studies from the University of Southern Maine. She has a strong passion for awakening awareness in others and guiding them along their own self-healing journey.

Becky currently resides in Maine and lives with her partner, Abel and their daughter, Lucy. She is also a stepmom to two amazing children, Pacific and Phoebe, who are now grown and living their own beautiful lives. After having Lucy in March of 2020, she felt a strong desire to write what she is teaching her daughter. This is where her first book and her "Little Healers" book series started. Becky hopes to bring the teachings of reiki, chakras, energy healing, children's mindfulness, meditation for children and much more into your home.

When Becky isn't immersed in her healing work or writing, she loves spending time with family and friends, being in nature, going for long walks, listening to music and cooking for her family.

Email: hello@littlehealers.net

Websites:
www.littlehealers.net
 www.beckysskincareandbodywork.com
Facebook Pages:
https://www.facebook.com/littlehealersbookseries
https://www.facebook.com/beckysskincareandbodywork
Instagram:
@little_healers
@beckysskincareandbodywork

# ELEVEN

## Alexandra Hanly

### DESERT AWAKENING: THE NEW DAWN OF AN OLD SOUL

I must admit that writing this chapter was not the easiest experience. I ran into energetic blocks, past life wounds, ancestral plights, and more. Cue the confetti for thriving through another inescapably tumultuous spiritual deep dive. My fellow spiritual seekers out there know what I mean. I'm talking about those kinds of spiritual experiences that you're not at all expecting, turn you out on your ass, and transform you into a wiser, braver, and more evolved version of yourself —whether you want to or not. Tune back in next week for the sequel, The Art of Panicking Discretely While Navigating Writing-Induced Dark Nights of The Soul, by Alexandra Hanly.

I became so befuddled with writer's block that I went to the Akashic Records to have a sit down with some famous writers who have transitioned beyond the veil and received wonderful advice (one author was quite fond of using a Salmon swimming upstream as an analogy). Yet still, every time I sat down to write I felt like my words became distorted, discontent little spiders who would much prefer to scurry off to the dark corners of the world or even surrender to the sweet release of the *delete* button rather than continue to be subjected to the chaotic barrage of half-baked thoughts that became my computer screen.

When I first started to write this chapter, I felt unable to communicate even to a level of *minimal* satisfaction, and this was incredibly frustrating because I thought I could write fairly well considering I minored in English in College (I have a suspicion that most English minors believe they write well, though). My English advisor told me that I had the makings of an author and I think I took this to mean that it would be easy to write a book. I have learned, yet again, that all because you are meant for something does not mean that it will be easy.

While all of this so far may sound like I have a self-defeating attitude, it is simply me having a good laugh after finally feeling the magic of my words come together on these pages. Afterall, the fish-fond author in the Akashic records did tell me that this was all meant to be fun and not to take life too seriously.

What happened to me while writing this chapter, I am still not entirely sure. I knew I was meant to contribute here, especially once I saw one of my spirit animal guides on the cover. It was not an easy birthing, but it was never meant to be. It took the struggle against the word-spiders to realize that I needed to start this chapter in an unconventional way.

That way is to address you now, dear reader, before I go into any stories or more flowery-worded ponderings. Because I have an important message for you. The purpose of me writing this chapter I have realized is not about me, it is about *you*, the one reading these words right now. You are a very, very special soul.

If you have ever felt different, that is because you are.

You do not need to conform to be happy.

Different does not mean that you are alone.

You have never been and will never be alone.

*You are powerful.*

You have a purpose.

You are a powerful being and you are reading this book, this chapter, these words, right now because you have a calling. *You* are special. Not everyone will read these words, so they are not meant for everyone. *You* are special and the world *needs you* and your unique magic. We need you to come alive in your rawest authenticity. We need to hear your childlike laughs, your soulful roar, your pounding heartbeat.

Let passion and curiosity for your next breath inspire you. Let freedom motivate you.

Grant your soul permission to heal itself with autonomous bravery, while accepting support from souls-alike. Gleaming vessels of conscious illusion are we, like ships in the night, navigating through an upward stream of noise, pain, love, and memories that comprise this shared planetary experience.

The lemon grove that is our heart-space is lush, bright, and fragrant. Yet, the storms do come—watering our roots, but at the cost of momentary fear. The fruit of our labors nourish us but not before recoiling our muscles with the manifested essence of sour. To relish the eventual sweetness, we must bear the initial discomfort. We ought not attach to either.

You are being called to awaken interdimensionally, to come alive in every atom of your being. Hear the universe sing to you in your own private tongue, inviting your bones to dance like petition cards in the wind, leaving behind them a wake of encoded memory for generations to come. We are the vanguard of the awakening movement in this era. It is not an easy calling – yet, we have agreed to it.

For all the times you felt unseen, unnoticed, unloved, and unappreciated—shatter the walls of these memories with your guttural call of release. We hear you.

Every time you have felt crazy, lost, misunderstood—let that be the kindling beneath your fire and become the beacon for all those who have felt the same, for we are legion! We are not alone in these feelings nor in this journey. More will join us; light the way.

I see us awakened souls dancing at the bonfire of this shared heart-space, warming and comforting one another, fading in and out of the human-conditioned oscillation of oneness back to self-identity.

Whatever your journey has been, no matter the struggles that you have faced and the demons that you have overcome and the battles you still fight—you are here, and I love you for it. I see you. In my own way, yes, I *do* see you. I feel every reader who comes across these pages, because the words upon them are a part of my soul.

There are no mistakes, no coincidences. Reading this book right now means something. What it means is up to you. Perhaps you will experience the comfort of solidarity in my words. Maybe you will see a way out of a dark place by reading how I found the illumined doors to my own liberation. Maybe you will feel the love and healing energy that I have infused into every word in this chapter and *that* will be enough. See this as your sign to step into your true calling. To finally say NO to the things that do not serve you and YES to your authentic soul-purpose. No matter where you are in life, you are exactly where you are meant to be.

━━━

I WAS BORN into this lifetime a beautiful shade of Shiva blue.

I was delivered by emergency c-section with a dangerously low heart rate due to the umbilical cord being wrapped around my neck five times to a mother who had been told by doctors that she could never conceive in the first place.

It is said that we are born into the world exactly as we departed from the last one. From everything I have seen and experienced beyond the veil, I believe that in between incarnations we spend time (can you call it *time* in the ethers?) "resting in the cosmos." When we are birthed, we come back in a similar way of how we left the previous life, regardless of how "long" we were resting in the ethers betwixt our terrestrial embodiments.

In that resting period, we decide who we will be, where and when we will live, and who our families will be.

I have lived over seven thousand human incarnations on Earth.

How do I know this? From information gleaned within the Akashic Records.

Without any prior knowledge I have discovered names, places, and stories about my past lives in the Akashic Records which have been confirmed with post-research. I have my qualms with the rising dangers of technology but as a natural born skeptic I am thankful for Google. Without having the internet to substantiate my findings, I would have never believed any of it. To go into meditation, hear names, experience events, and then return to see it all verified—it is bewildering.

To understand the Akashic Records, or "Hall of Records," we must first recognize the elemental building blocks of all things manifest in this dimension—earth, water, fire, air, and ether. Ether is also called space or "akasha" in Sanskrit, and it is the most subtle of all elements. It holds all information of the uni(multi)verse and is described as, "the breath of the Gods." Everyone is believed to have a "soul book" which holds every detail of each incarnation. The Akashic Records is beyond time and contains the wisdom of every-thing that has ever happened and will happen, as well as every thought and feeling.

The Akashic Records is a conceptualized interdimensional "place," within the ether that can be reached through meditation, psychic abilities, or astral travel. The realm is filled with guides, ascended masters, and record keepers. If you are familiar with Edgar Cayce, the "sleeping prophet," he conducted his readings by retrieving Akashic Records.

As a child I was able to access the realms beyond effortlessly, but as societal programming restructured my mind with machine-like conditioning, a matrix-loomed wool was pulled over my eyes and my abilities became inaccessible and undesirable. I started my life a *believer* but by the time I reached college, all that I placed my beliefs in were numbers and statistics.

After graduating college I moved to New York and went into modeling. My mid-late twenties were a pitch-black dark night of my soul. The reason that I made it out as the person I am today even though the odds became stacked against me is because I have a mission to fulfill. In those gloomy days that became months and then years, there came a point that I no longer recognized myself—I was completely lost. I did not have faith in a higher power (even though I wanted to) so I lived through my body and not from my soul. People who function from their bodily shells become slaves to the seeking of pleasure and avoidance of pain. People who are disconnected from their souls succumb to addictions of substances, adrenaline, stimuli, sex, money, and the like. They become wholly ensnared within the system of the illusionary matrix. We are *programmed* to be trapped in this figmented prison…some of us break free.

After a certain point, I had enough of living recklessly and I knew things needed to change. As my dear late friend, Dave, would say, nothing changes if nothing changes. I went to a Disney audition in Manhattan for what I thought was a Princess role but turned out to be for dancers on the cruise ships. I am no dancer. There are some incredible dancing schools in Manhattan and I feel like every dance student scurried out in swarms to that audition. They said absolutely no one should be there who wanted to audition for a Disney Princess—but I was never one for following rules. I decided to stay through it and just laughed at myself as I sadly tried to follow along. When I could not keep up with the choreography, I would stand in good humor, smile, and wave like the Queen of England. Somehow, I made it down to the final cut. Not long after the audition fiasco, I received a call from the head of the international casting office who told me to choose which park I would like to relocate to so I could play Elsa. I was informed that this was the first time they paid to relocate a new hire across the country to play a princess role.

I believed that a change in geography would help me, but I still felt lost in California. I would have been misplaced anywhere, though, because what was missing was my connection to Spirit; I was soul-sick. I did not understand the spiritual nature of my problem at the time so I just partied through it, believing that at some point I would miraculously snap out of it. I was in a lot of pain, and I did not know how to make it stop.

My good friend at the time asked me to go to a yoga festival with them.

"Nope, no thanks, not my scene." I immediately told him.

As his friend, I eventually agreed to accompany him to Joshua Tree for the five-day festival.

I never saw anything like it, it was not my world. The endless yoga classes, foreign music, CBD drizzled avocado toast, clouds of frank-incense, tables upon tables of expensive *rocks*. All of it was way over my head. These were not my people—*yet*.

It felt as if anyone we bumped into asked if we were going to see Michael Brian Baker from The Breath Center. Who? What? Huh? It was some sort of breathing session I was informed and, "you just can't miss it, sis, it's *soooo* deep."

It seemed like every acai-bowl eating, cacao drinking, ecstatic drum dancing, and lotus sitting yogi at that festival was going to Michael Brian Baker's workshop. My friend wanted to be one of them. We had been forewarned by the "helpful hippies" (that is how I naively perceived these generally wonderful people at the time) to get in line unreasonably early if we wanted a good chance of being admitted. My friend and I agreed to meet in line 3 hours before the doors opened. I waited in that hot desert sun for over three hours and my friend never made it.

"Well, now what?" I thought, panicking.

Deciding that I was not going to leave after spending my whole afternoon in line, I stayed put. Eventually, they announced they were letting us in, and it felt like I was watching people frenzy to the last Furby on Christmas Eve in 1998. I was one of the last two people in.

The cathedral-ceilinged music hall was *packed*…and *hot*. It was noisy and a diverse sampling of sweat offerings wafted on varying currents of air; essence a la' sardine-packed yogis.

The hall was quieted, and we were instructed to lay down on our yoga mats. I did not have one.

I found a place on outskirts of the circular room and stuffed my legs uncomfortably beneath a bench along the wall. I was nauseous from the huge burrito I shoved down my gullet right before this and felt as if I had a thirst that would never subside.

The commotion in the hall softened and Michael started speaking. I was taken aback by how humble he was. He spoke quietly, with gratitude, with…*awe*. I understand now that this is a man who consistently approaches life with the beginner's mind.

Settled nervously on the hard floor and flanked between two slippery, sweaty shoulders, I listened closely to the pranayama breathing instructions. The music began and so did my breath. This is not a sweet, gentle calming breath—this is a breath that *awakens*.

Across the vast room I began to hear people cry, then laugh, then scream and *howl*. I could not believe my ears.

I thought, "I am surrounded by loonies. These people are fucking nuts."

I could not hold back my rising chuckle despite how hard I tried. As I erupted in laughter, I noticed that there were streams of tears like salt rivers flowing down my cheeks and pooling into my ears, making my neck sticky. I did not realize before that point that I had been crying. Something was happening to me.

I stayed with the breath.

I felt like every ounce of pain, hurt, regret, and shame, pooled into my heart and appeared before my closed eyes as beams of light. Forgiveness drowned me, and I welcomed the flood that suffocated out the hatred, pain, confusion, and grief.

So much pain.

Generations of pain. Lifetimes of it. Accumulated and piled together all in this moment. It came before me in a way that I could —in just one breath—forgive and release oceans worth of throbbing heartache as if it had never belonged to me.

Gone.

Suddenly, I was in the body of a woman in an ancient civilization, harvesting red clay from the side of a mountain. The urgency and stress that I felt in her body was beyond anything I have ever felt in this one. I felt true fear-based survival instincts, scarcity of resources, and limited means for communication. I realize this was one of the first civilizations on earth.

After this experiential glance into antiquity, I was pulled up and away from earth. I settled into a red nebula and was cradled in the cosmos. I *was* the cosmos; a titanic of conscious stardust floating in a sea of tranquil darkness. I was home.

Knowledge engulfed my mind beyond anything I can even begin to explain. I was having samadhi, nirvana, enlightenment. In that moment of full gnosis, I downloaded an interminable treasure trove of universal wisdom. I was the infinite, and my knowing was limitless.

The following account is my best explanation of how the universe works from what I learned during gnosis, the complete spiritual knowing of perceived ultimate Truth.

There is one source energy. People call this God, Spirit, The Divine, Brahman, etc. Let us call it the One. This One expanded and created duality, which is Manifest existence. The One, through means of The Manifest, divided itself into even more expressions so that it could experience itself. I will call these primordial conscious expressions as an entire unit the Collective Consciousness but sometimes it is referred to as *Universal Consciousness* or *Paramatman.*

Each individualized expression of consciousness within the collective is like a large soul. I will call this an "Oversoul," but sometimes you will hear it referred to as *Higher Self, Eternal Self,* or *Atman.* Oversouls are of different "ages" depending on when they become their own conscious expression and the One continues to create new expressions even now. Which is why you sometimes hear the terms old soul and new soul. I used to think that the "age" of a soul depended strictly on experience, however, it has to do with experience *and* creation. Understanding soul genesis is a bit of a mind bender—put simply, time works differently in the ethers. To us, it appears to be linear, but it is not that simple. It *can* be linear, but it is also not. Regardless of "when" Oversouls come into being, the essence of each Oversoul is still from the same archaic One. Every Oversoul, no matter the age, is equally important and all-knowing.

When an Oversoul decides to have an incarnation, it takes a parcel of itself and puts it inside a temporary vessel. We will call this piece the Soul, which is sometimes referred to as the *Ego, Self,* or in Sanskrit as *Jiva-Atman.* In other words, the Oversoul—which is an individualized expression of Manifest consciousness from the One —takes from itself a seed of consciousness (Soul) and puts it within a body or avatar to live out a temporary incarnation. Understanding this, we can deduce that the Soul comes directly from One. The Soul is One. Atman is Brahman. You are God.

I felt the presence of other Oversouls in my cosmic home, however, we were not in each other's vicinity. Telepathic knowing and universal intercommunication (the interbeing), made us aware of one another, but there was a sense of being "far away." I was embraced by silent, infinite darkness that was anything but empty. Within that darkness was pure potentiality and absolute *love.* Not the kind of love that gives you butterflies, but the kind that feels like a blanket of sublime and infinite peace.

Moments from my past and current lives converged and pirouetted around the fringes of my awareness, flickering reels of bygone memories and lessons displayed in equal and present time. I peered down on earth as if it were a chessboard drawn on a buoyant beach ball, requiring calculated moves from each player who enlisted.

We are not conscious of our Oversoul in the same way that it is aware of us, owing to an amnesiac spell cast over our human form. When we assume our temporary avatar, we are forced to forget because the rules of the incarnation game require that we play without our infinite wisdom. Our Oversoul watches us patiently from the cosmos until we return to it and our memories are restored. When we have no players on the board we rest, strategize, and decide upon the next figure we will present as. Each time you play the game, you learn more until you have mastered it and no longer need to return—this is called *moksha*—liberation from incarnation.

I downloaded an immeasurable amount of information when I went back home to my Oversoul, cradled in the cosmos. In addition to being enlightened about the Universal inner workings which I recounted above, I also discovered that not every human body has a soul within it. This disturbed me and I did not tell anyone about my discovery for a long time until I heard Doloros Cannon call these individuals "backdrop people."

I wonder if Shakespeare experienced Samadhi enlightenment because he was right, the whole world *is* a stage. The entire *multiverse* is a theater filled with interdimensional players often participating in a game which they are unaware.

I felt myself being tugged back to the 3D world, but I resisted the familiar pull of gravity, knowing that Earth and other similar planets were distorted projections of The Truth. I did not want to return only to once again be spellbound within a body that is trapped in an illusionary matrix. I knew that once I fully resumed my human form, I would be swept back into the game.

When I reoccupied my physical body, I walked outside to an orange sun lazily casting elongating shadows over the cacti of Joshua Tree, creating a sandy sea of sundials.

Michael was outside, all in white and surrounded by people. I walked up to him, shaking like a stack of unsteady teacups.

I managed, shakily, "thank you, *thank you*."

His face looked as if he were the one approaching me in gratitude and he said with eyes full of sincerity, "you are so powerful."

With those four words, self-doubt dissolved like a dusty timeworn ribbon falling away from an old forgotten package.

I could speak no more.

I walked out to the desert and continued walking.

I wanted to keep walking to the edge of the world until I fell off and back into the stars again.

When I regained my ability to speak, I called my mom and felt deeply understood. I was born into a family that supports and loves me unconditionally and I thank the universe for that every day. Even though I do feel an intense longing to reunite again with my Oversoul, there is so much here I love and am grateful to experience. I am in love with life.

I moved back to the east coast and went up to Vermont to be with my parents. Divine orchestration still at work, a yoga studio opened just down the road from me.

I could not unsee what I experienced in my awakening, and I had no choice but to follow the spiritual path. Initially, it was a hard transition. I felt like Dr. Jekyll and Mr. Hyde. My true identity had been awakened, but my habitual self was ignoring the eviction notice. I fought with my two halves, going back and forth in constant conflict. I would cry, wishing to become one again with who I knew I truly was.

I expressed these concerns to my yoga teacher, Angie Follensbee-Hall. She told me something which planted the seed of bourgeoning hope that would keep me going on this path until my physical self caught up with the spiritual.

She told me a story from the film *Awake* about Paramahansa Yogananda. In the movie, a devotee recounts a conversation with Yogananda wherein he asks the guru what was not permitted while studying with him.

Yogananda asks the man, "Do you smoke cigarettes?"

The man answers, "yes."

Yogananda replies, "You can do that."

Yoganadanda then asks him, "Do you drink alcohol?"

The man replies, "yes."

Yogananda says, "You can do that."

Then, Yogananda asks the man, "Do you have relations with the opposite sex?"

The man responds, "yes."

Yogananda says again, "You can do that. But, you may find that you do not want to do these things so much anymore."

That is exactly how it happened for me. I did not stop anything, I just kept showing up. I *added* to my life my devotion to spirituality and in time my life naturally course-corrected. The things that were no longer aligned with my soul organically fell away.

The reason I tell this story is for anyone who has had an awakening (or wants to). If you feel like you do not know how to proceed or even start, just keep showing up. Eventually, you will end up exactly where you are meant to be. Awakenings can happen in an instant, but it may take time for your life to catch up. Be patient, keep hope, and stay committed.

After a few years, I reached out to Michael, the person who facilitated my life-changing awakening. He offered to teach me privately, to show me the way to help awaken others. I was the first person he offered one-on-one training to for Anatomy of Awakening. I am forever grateful to him for awakening and mentoring me personally, and for all that he does to help the world as a whole.

I am still on my spiritual journey, and I do not believe that ends for any of us until we return to the One. My subconscious has been purged of decades of programming, my psychic skills have been restored, and I now devote my life to helping animals and assisting people on their spiritual journeys. Helping animals is one of my primary missions and I have been able to support various animal charity organizations around the world through my spiritual work. I spend a lot of time in the Akashic Records as both a reader and an Akashic Architect$^{SM}$, creating etheric environments for my students to heal and grow. I have downloaded energetic codes called The Awakened Bliss Codes $^{SM}$ and train practitioners to effectively use these unique energies to support themselves and the collective consciousness. The codes are infused within this chapter.

My advice to anyone reading this is to keep going and put your whole heart into this life. Live with unapologetic love, humor, ferocity, and compassion. Question *everything* that looks like conformity or societal programming. You have a purpose. You *are* special. You are loved. As my mentor told me years ago, *you* are powerful.

I want to thank my family, the most amazing group of people an Oversoul could ever choose to incarnate with—I love you more than any word-spiders can express on paper. I express deep gratitude to my many mentors and teachers on this plane and beyond. I extend love to my friends and am forever grateful to the one who took me to that yoga festival. I thank my guides and The Council in the Akasha who guide me in my life and in my writing. I thank those who I have lost in this realm but still support me in spirit. I thank my ancestors of earth, blood, and stars. I thank Source—there are no words for my love and gratitude. Finally, I thank you, dear reader, for sharing your time and energy here in this ink and paper portal with me. May we one day meet again.

I depart from these pages with the following words from Douglas Adams, "I may not have gone where I intended to go, but I think I ended up where I needed to be."

## About the Author

### ALEXANDRA HANLY

Alexandra Hanly is a Chief Spiritual Advisor and creator of the leading-edge Awakened Bliss Codes<sup>SM</sup> energy technology channeled directly from the Akashic Records. She is an internationally known Energetics Expert, Akashic Records Architect<sup>SM</sup>, Multigenerational Psychic-Medium, and Intuitive Healer. She has extensive yogic and Vedic knowledge and has studied with the most highly regarded and influential spiritual authorities in the world. She earned her BA in Clinical and Counseling Psychology in 2011 from The College of New Jersey on full scholarship and holds a vast array of holistic healing and spiritual certifications.

Alexandra founded Grace Through Gravity (GTG) to empower humanity and guide spiritual leaders, energy workers, healing practitioners, and higher-self seekers on their paths to bliss and holistic wellness across the globe. She teaches practitioners, executives, thought leaders, and empowered individuals through exclusive 1:1 private spiritual advisement, expert small group consulting, and online spiritual programs. Her overall mission is to help animals and support as many souls as possible in reaching their highest life purpose. As a passionate believer in compassion for all souls, GTG is proud to contribute a minimum of 11% of all proceeds to animal charities.

She hails from NYC and was raised in New Jersey. She now lives in Vermont with her beloved border terrier, Piper, and her family (who are her best friends).

Website: www.gracethroughgravity.com

IG: @alexandra_h_h

Clubhouse: @alexandragtg

Facebook Personal: facebook.com/unicornalexandra1/

Facebook Group: facebook.com/groups/spiritualitysupport/

Facebook Business: facebook.com/gracethoughgravity

# TWELVE

# Jessica Verrill

---

## BETWEEN THE SHADOWS

I rolled over in bed and opened my eyes. It was perhaps 8:30 in the evening, I had just snuggled my beautiful daughter to sleep and had dozed off like I often do from the quiet comfort of her breathing and heart connected to mine. Bedtime is one of my favorites as we connect about our day, have some laughs, and sometimes tears. This night was like any other. As I woke, the light was shining in from the hallway and illuminated the room softly. My gaze landed on the face and shoulders of a young man above me. As I connected in, he smiled, turned his head, and began to move away from the bed until he disappeared.

I lay in bed, taking in what had just happened. I took note of how utterly calm and peaceful I felt, something that I was not sure I would feel with my first experience of seeing a spirit with my physical eyes in many years. I am trained and experienced in compassionate depossession and psychopomp work, as well as decades of training and practicing different forms of healing, trance, channeling, and psychic work. I am very adept at sensing, hearing and working with the spirit realm, and, it's not something I was ready to experience in this way before now. There were a lot of fears that needed to be worked through and a lot of strengthening of boundaries.

## Boundaries.

If I had one thing to strongly advise anyone experimenting, working in, or wanting to work in the energetic and spiritual realms, it would be to learn how to develop and enforce strong boundaries—in all areas of your life. It can make an enormous difference in your experiences and the trajectory of your life, and your spiritual connection.

When I was in some of my trainings for deep work like curse removal, past life work, and depossession, some of the participants were having challenges with things like spiritual interference, not being able to sleep, and a bunch of other obnoxious paranormal occurrences. This clearly mimicked the challenges with boundaries in other areas of their life as well, so it was not a skill they had learned and could translate to this area. I don't know about you, but being woken from sleep and disturbed in my daily life by those wanting my help or support, is not something I'm okay with, and so I don't allow it. I am not available for my clients, in the spiritual or physical realms, during certain times or places, including when I'm sleeping, spending time with family, and just like I wouldn't allow a client to show up on my doorstep unannounced, I don't allow it from spirits.

When looking at your current boundaries and how to strengthen them think of things around when and how do you want to be.

Do you have certain hours that you are open to work—including client conversations, responding to emails, etc. that you generally adhere to?

How do you handle requests outside of that?

In what ways are you open for communication?

In regards to spirits, what energies are you willing to work with?

Do you check in regularly with the integrity of your guides?

What experiences are off-limits to you?

For example, I'm not open to working with guides that are less than a 9 out of 10 in integrity. I check this regularly, especially before channeling or seeking guidance or working with clients through muscle testing. Any guide that is less than that is commanded to leave, as I am not interested in working with anyone but the highest guidance. It opens up more possibilities for lower vibrational inter-ference and skewing of my work. This is also something really important to note when receiving sessions from other people. If you are allowing your energy to be accessed by this person and their guides, be sure that you are aware and comfortable with who and how they are connecting with.

I have had boundaries around anything in my bedroom, outside of certain hours, and I am off-limits to seeing energies that are of lower vibration at this time. Recently, I changed my boundaries a bit and asked to see some of my ancestors and guides at any time and intu-itively knew it would be in that state between waking and sleep when we are more present and open.

We have access to these realms all of the time. Some of us have been raised in a way that we are naturally able to keep our lines of connection open, and many of us have not. We may have beliefs, energies, or other influences that prevent us from being aware of and working with these innate abilities. It can take a lot of work and persistence to allow these abilities expression in our lives.

One morning, while attending a class for my herbal apprenticeship, we were learning and connecting with Bee Balm. I had just been gifted some of these plants a few months prior, but working with plants in this way was a deepening of previous studies and one that I had yet to explore much. In this moment, as I tuned into these plants, I was given images of working with community and the importance of it. I heard the plant talking and could feel the healing vibration within. It was such a powerful experience and one that opened me up to a whole new level of working with nature.

For many years I trained to access wisdom, guidance, and healing through a journey or trance-like state. It was done in a very ceremonial way, with steps such as grounding, charging your energy up, and listening to rhythms that guide you into this trance. Once there, you connect with your different validated helping spirits and animals to partner up for the benefit of the client, situation or experience intended. At times, I would receive information about working with the energy or medicine of certain plants, but doing so without the ceremonial steps was a new experience for me.

In sessions with clients, I found myself entering this trance-like state without all the to-do. Information and healing streamed out of me. Not of me, but through me. Guidance came in, tones expressed and eventually I began to speak what I now know to be Light Language, or the language of our soul. I was conscious to the experience and integrity of what was coming through, but would not be able to recall the details of what was shared even hours later. This is also the time, that connecting in with my star family happened and I felt strongly that I needed to be a bridge between the advanced healing and technology available in the quantum field and grounding it into the earth and this existence. I received intense healings and energetic body upgrades through this connection, that I knew was intended to strengthen my foundation and open more gifts.

I dove into studying and creating flower essences, vibrational essences of things like the solar eclipse, and eventually had the nudge to channel the energetic properties of a tree to help a friend with a particular situation we had been trying to fully release over a couple of sessions together. I leaned into the Hawthorn tree I was working with and felt it pulsate through me. I had my friend's prior permission and began to direct this frequency towards her. I began to see this situation dismantling, and the remaining pieces we had not previously been able to access cleared away. As the flow continued, I saw protection over her, and healing of her heart transmitted. With the assistance of this magnificent tree, we were able to unlock the final piece needed for her to regain her energy, clear this from her energetic field, and release any ties to the other person in other lifetimes and realities. For her, this was an extremely powerful session. For me, this was next level embodiment and intertwining of these different facets of healing I have explored.

As I continue to interact with the spirits of the plants, I have been guided to offer more transmissions of this potent energy to facilitate healing to anyone or anything around the world. The plants a lot to say and love to share immense wisdom if we are able to slow down and trust what we are receiving. When I say my world has opened up from this, it has given me an insider perspective on nature. I regularly check-in with my plants to see how they are doing, if there is anything they need or request and build a relationship to them, much like I would my animal or human companions. Animals are much more complex and while it's a beautiful skill to communicate with them directly, my dog is typically reminding me I didn't feed her or asking to play fetch and my cat typically wants to be let outside or is negotiating more time outside before coming in for the night.

I'm not unique in these abilities, I truly believe everyone has this potential. What I have that others may not, is commitment to my energetic and spiritual development—really my personal development, as it encompasses all areas for me. I am committed to growth and motivated for and by it. As we learn to access the realms that are beyond the veil, we bring in more support for our growth. It's not all love and light—which is really spiritual bypassing, or using spiritual practices to bypass your feelings—to promote that. In reality, there are hard feelings to experience, shadows to integrate, and initiations to experience, all of which add depth and power to ourselves.

Often, when we embrace and fully integrate the pieces of us that are "too much", make ourselves or others uncomfortable, we find our deepest gifts. For so long, I tried to dismiss or ignore my anger that I felt for most of my life until I realized, that anger is not something to put out, but to direct into the things that I'm most angry about: societal structures and programs that don't serve most, child endangerment, human trafficking, and animal rights. My anger isn't the problem, it can serve as fire or passion for a solution, it's in the belief and the dismissing of this, that I'm attempting to cut off a necessary part of me. I'm not in this world to follow the status quo, but to bring in new ways of being and without identifying the problem areas, I'm not able to properly focus my energy on change.

There are dark forces that we neither want to feed or deny. It is necessary to be aware of these energies and do our internal work so that we have the strength to rise above and maintain our power, when we are faced with it. Many well meaning "love and light only" folks, cause harm to themselves and others by denying the fact that these energies exist. It is not serving anyone—not themselves, not their clients, and not the collective. There is a polarity in everything, where there is light, there must be dark, and this is where having very strong boundaries, connection with your guides and regularly checking the integrity of them is of utmost importance. While, "good vibes only" can be a great reminder to stay positive, in grati-tude, and focus on what you want to create, the potential for spiri-tual bypassing is tremendous. I will note that maintaining a high energetic frequency can help your experience with any of these denser forces, but done through deep healing and alchemizing your traumas, instead of stuffing them down and putting on a smile while you chant.

One of my dearest mentors used to say, 'It's not what you do, it's who you become," meaning through your spiritual work. The impact that we have when we heal ourselves is rippled into every interaction, it serves to raise the collective vibration and allows us to focus more energy on creation of the new earth or living in such a way that is supportive the majority. We don't all need to quit jobs and careers we love to pursue a business as a psychic, healer, or coach. In fact, please don't, if you're not feeling that deep pull of these professions. In reality, we need there to be those having posi-tive impact and interaction within all areas of society: real estate, retail, restaurant, and everything else. If waiting tables feeds your soul and learning to read the akashic records for your own enjoy-ment feels like the perfect balance, you are doing a great service (no pun intended) to all of the patrons, co-workers and employers you interact with. The same is for anywhere. In become a more healed, whole version of yourself, you need not do anything more, you have become exactly who you need to be.

In all of my containers, whether for writing, publishing, energetic, group, or 1:1, my underlying goal is always to connect you more deeply into your personal power and guidance system. As we move through the layers of trauma, emotional residue, mindset issues, unhealthy belief systems, and energetic debris, attachments or leaks, we begin to free up more energy to feed our power, genius and gifts. Every single time we release something no longer serving us, we add to our momentum and increase our vibrational frequency. This is key for manifesting, creation, being present, and enhancing our internal compass that will lead us to creating lives that we feel aligned to in our body, mind and soul.

You can begin to move through some of this by bringing in more consciousness into your life. Start to become aware of the ways you react during the day, your overall experience, and tune closely into what feels like it drains your energy. Do you feel triggered by your child crying? There is likely some much needed healing needed around your experience of crying as a child. In these moments, practice breathing, bringing yourself back to center, and reminding yourself you are safe. Empathize with your child and remember what feels insignificant to you can be a tremendous source of pain or upset for a still developing child.

Perhaps you want to build your business but every time you go to post online or do a live video, you freeze up, feel like you're going to vomit, and have the sudden urge to run off to live in the forest. What is the worst thing that's going to happen? Get to the bottom of this feeling and keep digging. Often, when we dive in, it may start something like this, "People are going to judge me and know I'm a fraud. My clients won't want to keep working with me, I won't have any money to pay my bills. I'll have to try to find a job. What if I can't?? What will I do?? I'll lose my home and everything I've worked so hard for. I'll be homeless and my kids will be taken because I can't care for them." All from a live video. Hmmm. Usually when you get to the bottom of this narrative, something shifts. You have allowed fear to have its voice and, in the process, you hear how ridiculous it sounds and you move on. This isn't the end-all-be-all solution, but it's a great one to begin facing your fears and taking your power back from them.

Through writing and speaking about ourselves, our gifts, and our businesses, there are very often huge amounts of stuff to work though. When I offer courses in writing, or publishing, I offer strong energetic support as in everything I do, but it truly is a huge healing journey. Imposter syndrome comes up. You don't feel safe. There are issues with visibility and being seen. You're worried about being judged. It goes on and on. If you really want to dive into some deep healing quickly, commit to writing a book or a chapter in a book like this one!! It's sure to dredge up a lot you weren't aware of. On the other side is clarity, more confidence, enhanced authority, and a solid conviction in yourself. It has the potential to bring you so many more gifts and epiphanies than any journaling prompt ever could and for a personal development junkie, like myself, I love anything that is going to bring me closer to myself, my true self, as in my higher soul self.

What brings your closer to your higher soul self? Follow this, tune in, do the hard work and be compassionate with yourself through the process. It's not going to be easy, but I can tell you freeing your-self of the outdated programs, energetic debris, attachments, and limiting beliefs will truly allow you to energy and ability to create a life that you love as well as help raise the frequency of the collective. Thank you. Much love.

## About the Author

### JESSICA VERRILL

Jessica Verrill is an energetic alchemist, intuitive channel and USA Today Bestselling Author. As the founder of House of Indigo, a multimedia publishing company, she supports spiritual leaders in sharing their unique gifts and teachings to elevate their authority.

Her skills as an intuitive coach and energetic alchemist supports high levels of growth and alignment, while working directly as a channel to her personal guides. As a life-long learner, she is often immersed in books and classes, including all aspects of herbalism and flower essences, health, wellness and personal development, spirituality, and enhanced psychic development.

Jessica lives in Maine with her husband, daughter, black lab and cat —a new addition to her family that showed up in the yard. She loves gardening, communing with nature spirits, hiking, exploring nature, being around water, traveling and personal development.

Email: publishing@jessverrill.com
Websites: jessverrill.com, house-indigo.com
Facebook Page:
https://www.facebook.com/HouseOfIndigoPublishing
Facebook Group:
https://www.facebook.com/groups/indigoinitiative/
Instagram: @Jess.Verrill
Clubhouse: @JessVerrill

THIRTEEN

# Kinsey Kahlo

EXPLORING AND HEALING THE SUBCONSCIOUS FOR
DEEP TRANSFORMATION

Dear Reader, you are a beloved multi-dimensional being of light who is layered from your most basic design of the human body to a formless and luminous Being of Light. You are a creator being, and the quality, or meaning, of your human life is dependent upon your willingness to experience all levels of you.

You came into this life with an intention to have a truly human experience. Inherent to the experience of a human being is an Egoic "self" identification. You are not meant to be only a being of "love and light" because you are also a being of dense form and creation. From the very cells of your body to the higher consciousness of your Higher Self, all parts of you are valid and worthy of your Divine, unconditional love.

Many spiritual teachers talk about "killing the ego" or guide others to avoid or escape the pains of the human experience. This is a great oversight of the real meaning in life. We are here to see, feel, and love all of it. All the parts of you that are broken, shamed, or hidden are here to be seen and felt into integration with your soul and to assist it in its expansion and union with all of creation.

At your core, you are a conscious creator. The question is whether you are truly aligned with this version of yourself or whether you have become so lost in a sea of human programming and subconscious reactions to life that you no longer recognize yourself as such.

Have you heard that the subconscious mind runs about 90-99% of your human experience?

If not, let me elaborate on the profundity of that statement. You are only aware of about 1-10% of the experiences you have. For the sake of physical survival, your conscious mind blocks 90+ percent of the information and experiences you have because this makes it easier for you to make quick decisions in survival situations. Consciousness involves the thoughts, feelings, and experiences in which you are aware and directly engaged. The subconscious mind is comprised of the remaining content from all your experience—past, present, and future. You are largely driven by your subconscious into the experiences of reactive behaviors, patterns of thought, emotions you experience, and even the pain you hold in your body.

Your subconscious mind holds within it all of you—from the mystical, magical being of light you are to the broken, shattered, shamed, and hidden skeletons of your past, present, and future. In the subconscious, you are all of this, across all times, dimensions, and realities—all at once. There is no such thing as linear time in the subconscious mind—it is eternal, and everything is happening right NOW. Within the subconscious mind, you can witness or experience yourself as fractals of you as a whole being.

For the sake of simplicity, I will refer to the Ego as if it were a singular entity, although it is made up of many parts and layers. For example, in Freudian psychology, the layers are called the Ego, the ID, and the Superego; however, this detail is unimportant to the larger understanding as they are all parts of the Ego (compared to the layers and parts of your higher dimensional aspects, which I am collectively referring to as the Higher Self). The Ego largely exists in your subconscious mind; although you are consciously aware of the aspects you identify with—your conscious thoughts, likes/dislikes, job, home, relationships, skills, and experiences that you deemed as having shaped you (as you know yourself to be).

The Ego fills up a lot of most people's conscious minds—the constant chatter of thoughts you experience are all generated by your Ego. It narrates your conscious experiences and judges them as good/bad experiences, and it generates nearly all of the other conscious thoughts you have. The Ego also has subconscious thoughts and beliefs—these would be beliefs you don't consciously process (everything from "the sky is blue" to "I'm a bad person"). This subconscious material forms most of how you see and interact with yourself, others, and life in general.

So often, we're attempting to change our patterns and feelings through the conscious mind, missing out on the deeper parts of us that need our attention and awareness. We struggle to make meaningful and lasting changes in our lives when we have this "outside-in" approach to creating change. The good news is that you can heal the "broken" parts of yourself by accessing your subconscious, consciously and lovingly.

My guides shared this very interesting view of the Ego in the subconscious mind:

If the Ego were a place, it would be much like a funhouse of magical mirrors in a carnival. The Higher Self is the version of you that takes form and walks into the funhouse, and it is also the one who designed the funhouse and everything in it. Strangely, as soon as you walk into this funhouse, you forget that you designed and made everything in it, and you also forget what you looked like before you got there. In this funhouse, the Ego is all the versions of you that you see in all the mirrors you come across.

As you walk through the funhouse of mirrors, you will see yourself reflected back in many distorted images. In some, you will like what you see, and in others, you may be horrified by your appearance. Some you may try to break, but when you pass by again, they are magically reassembled and intact. Among all these images of you, which are not you, you will experience many different emotional responses to the reflections as indicators of alignment (answering, in part, the question, "is this image anything like me?").

These emotions also indicate the level of acceptance and love you allow yourself to feel for these versions of you. In some cases, you will feel an absolute aversion to the images you see of yourself. You may turn a corner and suddenly surprise yourself with a seemingly "ugly" version of yourself—like an automatic/unconscious reaction you deem as "bad" or "wrong". You may even exclaim, "That's not me!" and you would be right and also wrong.

You are the being who is looking in the mirror, and yet, as the mirror reflects these distorted versions of you back to you, you take them personally because you have forgotten that you are not the image you see. You can hardly bring yourself to look at some of the images because they disturb you so deeply, whereas others you may look at with admiration or awe—each time forgetting that these are just images, not true representations of you. In fact, these images can even be internalized views of you that you take on from others who do not see the real you either, and you do this to feel safer in the environment you are in—to make sense of a senseless experience and to shield yourself from the pain of the dissonance therein.

For example, you may walk up to a certain mirror wherein you feel you are never quite enough. In this mirror, you see all the flaws, shortcomings, and failures, and as you stand before this mirror, the Egoic mind speaks of what you could have done better, what you should have done, or how you fell short. This mirror would represent your Inner Critic—a part of your Egoic human experience, often internalized by the experience of someone close who was critical of you. And while you may look at this mirror and want to shut it up or turn away, it always comes back as you make your way through the funhouse of mirrors.

The trouble is your Inner Critic is there to help you, and when we shut it up and turn it away, we dishonor not only the part of ourselves that chose to internalize the dialogue and aspects of others for our personal gain, but we dishonor the experience of being a human entirely.

If you had a very critical parent, for example, you likely chose to feed, develop, and grow a strong Inner Critic part of your Ego. As such, you will return to this mirror often, even though it upsets or even terrifies you—the subconscious guides you here because this strategy has worked before. This Inner Critic served you in so many ways, preventing you from being surprised and shocked by the hurtful things others would say and do in response to you. And so, you set out in your subconscious mind to create a part of you that would save you from the pain of rejection and criticism. What we often fail to realize, when we feel attacked or hurt by voice of the Inner Critic, is that this part has done its job and done its job well. While you endured the intense criticisms of your parents, for example, you became more and more adept at handling the pain and hurt it caused because of this part of the Ego.

The Ego is on a journey of development, growth, and expansion itself, much like that of the Higher Self/Soul. And so, while the strategy of criticizing yourself served you while you were young, as an adult, you may find that you are no longer willing to let the Inner Critic run your life. This brings up a lot of resistance because you see this part of you saying hurtful things to you; it's only natural, according to the human experience of Ego, that we avoid pain and seek pleasure, so you turn away and shut it up. But we haven't updated the Ego with a new strategy, so the part/mirror comes back over and over. The counter-intuitive, yet effective, approach is in your willingness to go in—to connect with this part, to deeply love and accept this part of you, and to honor the strategies it employed to help you survive.

This is how we integrate the Ego: with the power of our love. As we stare at this image of our Inner Critic and allow it to be heard and felt, we can transmute the images of the part—reforming the mirror itself. Sometimes the best course of action is to melt the mirror and reuse the materials (this would be the integration of the Egoic part into the Higher Self). Sometimes the best course of action is to give the part a new job—perhaps instead of an Inner Critic, this part becomes the Cheerleader, for example. Through our love and appreciation of the part's skills and loving application of its desire to assist us in navigating the pains and joys of life, we can encourage it to release its old strategies that no longer serve us and to try new ways of interacting with us and the world.

These parts of you want nothing more than to help you survive and thrive. They are not your enemies; they are just misinformed. Through the pains and traumas of your life, your Ego formed false conclusions about you or about life itself, thus forming these distorted images of you. For example, a part of you may have decided when you were young and heavily criticized, "I can't do anything right." And this false conclusion (or limiting belief) got stored deep inside your subconscious—now spanning your past, present, and future—shaping your experience of yourself and life.

This belief may generate feelings of sadness, hopelessness, or desperation. Many different strategies for coping with these intense emotions can emerge as a result. We may procrastinate or self-sabotage; we may distract ourselves or avoid our feelings in other ways. Whatever we do, we likely end up reaffirming the validity of the belief that we can't do anything right, and so we end up in a cycle of re-experiencing how imperfect we are, coming back to this mirror again and again.

This limiting belief will continue to exist so long as it is not looked at, felt, loved, and allowed to be—only then can it be released or reformed.

Every experience we have—be them thoughts, feelings, or physical experiences—is an extension of collective consciousness itself. And all of consciousness, all of existence, all of creation, all experiences want to be experienced fully. So often, these parts are created out of trauma wherein we are so shocked, overwhelmed, or scared by the feelings we experience that we shove them away, dissociate, or check out of the experience (leaving much of it unprocessed).

The human mind is programmed to store the strategies employed as "effective" when we have survived seemingly dangerous or life-threatening experiences; as such, the mind may come to the false conclusion that you survived that pain by avoiding it, and it will automatically employ these strategies again and again. The mind does not consciously recognize the experience was not fully experienced, so much of the experience is stored in the subconscious mind, unresolved—playing over and over again. Imagine that the child who came to that conclusion is still stuck, in the subconscious experience, in that very moment—trying to work out what happened and why.

We can witness proof of this in our "overreactions" to the life experiences we have. The typical Egoic response is to blame the experience (or people involved) for the feelings we have. Yet, the real reason you experience the intense emotions you do is because the experience touches the dense, unprocessed material of your subconsciously stored past hurts and traumas. The present experience touches an anchored pain inside of you, provoking you to feel some of the unprocessed emotions from the previous experience. In the subconscious mind, both the present experience and the past experience are happening simultaneously.

The strange truth here is that the person that seemingly initiated this cascade of intense emotions is a blessing to you; offering you an opportunity to go into the past pains held in the subconscious mind and heal those pains and false images of you. Until they touched this material, you were likely unconscious of the deeper wounding you still held within you. The key here is to feel the feelings you did not have the capacity or wherewithal to feel at the time of the original wounding.

This is a difficult experience to embody at times because you are asked to go into the pain instead of averting yourself from it. Feeling the pain is not about talking about it, distracting yourself by doing other things, or forcing yourself to feel lighter feelings or think lighter thoughts—that is spiritual bypassing. Attempting to escape the pain of life is the biggest mistake we can make. It is the pain, the darkness, emptiness, sorrow, anger, and hurt that gives life and meaning to the joy, expansion, love, and fulfillment we are all worthy of experiencing.

You are worthy of a life of meaning and purpose—no matter who you are, what you have done, or how broken you feel you may be. The truth is you are whole and complete in and of yourself. Again, you are the being who is looking at all these mirrors, and each of these mirrors represents how you see yourself in any given moment. As you walk through life, you're walking through the funhouse of mirrors, reflecting back to yourself, the beautiful, the ugly, the broken, and the heroic parts of you, your Ego.

Within the realms of the subconscious, you can heal past traumas, limiting beliefs, fractured parts of your Ego, and so much more. Today, I lead others into the realms of their subconscious by creating a safe, non-judgmental, and unconditionally accepting environment for them, showing them how to find this environment within themselves, and leading them into a gentle, guided medita- tion form of healing. In these sessions, the client is fully awake and aware, and they are put in the driver seat, with me as their wise and loving driving instructor. I know and trust in every one of my clients that they can heal themselves, and my job is simply to support their journey. I do not save or fix anyone because they are not broken (even if the mirror they stand in front of insists that they are); I just help them see where this mirror came from and dissolve it so that they can begin to see who they really are without all of the distorted images that have confused and shrouded them.

We can access the subconscious with the conscious mind in this way because we format the experience to essentially speak the language of the subconscious. The subconscious speaks to us in images, emotions, and physical sensations, and these pieces of information are often symbolic of greater knowings or realizations—for example —dreams hold these components. When we create a safe place in the subconscious, and we offer some suggestions for how the subconscious can engage to help us make sense of this symbolic information, the subconscious is happy to engage and offer incredibly insightful and deeply healing awareness to the conscious mind. This active engagement helps us safely feel and resolve the hidden parts, beliefs, and experiences that have kept us feeling stuck in patterns of thought, emotion, or behaviors that are no longer serving us.

This work is my passion because it changed my life and helped me find who I really am behind all the distorted images I had taken on to survive my life. I grew up in an abusive, alcoholic home where mental, emotional, verbal, and physical abuse were normalized and regular experiences. As a sensitive child, I was often overwhelmed by my environment and caretakers, such that I internalized much of my experiences as traumatic. As a result, I struggled for 30+ years with disordered anxiety, depression, and anger issues, and most of my childhood was blocked from my memory. I had also developed a very strong Inner Critic part that drove me to perfectionism, patterns of self-doubt, and negative self-talk that would only heighten my anxiety and depression.

I found clever ways of talking myself out of my feelings. I would bottle my feelings until I would explode in volatile and even violent reactions. I never let people see me struggle or feel weak, unless they happened to see me explode, and then I would be filled with shame and more validation that no one would love me if they saw the real me. Internally, my life felt like a consistent downward spiral, while the outside world saw me achieving and working hard at fitting in. No amount of praise or validation was ever enough because I could not and did not truly allow myself to receive it.

This dark spiral led me to a place where I had achieved the "American Dream" of owning a beautiful home, having a high-paying salary, and having a partner and two children (for me, 2 cats)—all by the age of 25, during the biggest recession since the "Great Depression"—and yet, every day, I woke up trying to practice gratitude by listing for myself the things I "should be" grateful for, while feeling absolutely empty inside. One of the darkest hours of my life was a period of months, before my awakening, where every day started with thoughts about suicide after failing to experience gratitude, and each day ended with me collapsing and crying in my closet. Something had to give...

In my awakening, I first became aware of my Higher Self, and it guided me into the realms of the subconscious to heal broken parts of me, release limiting beliefs that had plagued me, and rediscover who I truly am. After years of traditional therapies that had taken the "outside-in" approach and left me going in circles, always returning to my old patterns and pains, it was me who healed me by taking an "inside-out" approach instead. After the clearing of just a few of my core negative beliefs (ex: "something is wrong with me"), I was able to get off my medications and start healing and regulating my nervous system myself. I went from a life of pain, anxiety, and constant over-reactions to the life I have now, where most days feel like a blessing and joy to experience, all by doing this inner work in the subconscious realms. Changing my internal landscape changed my external landscape - how I see and interact with myself and the world.

Through the guidance of my Higher Self and Spirit Guides, I was able to open myself to a level of self-love and self-acceptance that the younger version of me never could have imagined. As I continue this work with myself and others, I find myself more and more at peace with the world and others. Today, my Spirit Team guides me to assist others to heal themselves from the inside-out. I now see myself as a Soul Warrior of the Subconscious—an honored guide who holds the light in the darkness for myself and others.

The name of the game here is LOVE. You are encouraged to love all parts of you so much that they want nothing more than to rejoin you in love, peace, and harmony. May your pain be felt and loved into integration with your Spirit, expanding and updating you and the wisdom of your inner being. If you are hurting, please know you are loved and worthy of goodness. From my heart to yours, I wish you all of the blessings life can offer.

## About the Author

### KINSEY KAHLO

Kinsey Kahlo is the founder of Pinnacle Healing, a woman-owned business dedicated to providing coaching and healing in service to a growing population of awakening and evolving beings. As an Intuitive Emotional Wellness Coach, she specializes in uncovering and healing core issues that negatively affect emotional wellness—helping clients overcome trauma, grief, depression, anxiety, and more—and assisting in awakening her clients to their own internal wisdom and healing powers.

As a Certified Cognitive Behavioral Therapy (CBT) Practitioner, ClearBeliefs Coach, Conscious Coding Practitioner, Reiki Master, Animal Communicator, and Angelic Healing Practitioner, Kinsey blends traditional and non-traditional methods together to offer holistic, integrative, and transformational healing for all beings.

Kinsey lives in Washington with her husband, in-laws, and animal companions. She loves being in nature, talking to plants and animals, meditating, channeling angels and celestial beings, and learning about all things psychological and metaphysical.

Website: https://pinnacle-healing.com/
Facebook:
https://www.facebook.com/pinnaclehealing1111/
Instagram:
https://www.instagram.com/pinnaclehealing1111

# FOURTEEN

# Sierra Grana

## SPIRITUAL WARFARE

Stop thinking you're special—you are, but so is everyone else. Sure this is a rough beginning to this section, but it's true. Every single person is gifted with 5D capabilities, it's just whether or not they want to unlock that door. Most don't out of fear of judgement, condemnation, and approval from others.

As children, we had very active and awakened third eyes, it's the aging process that hindered it for most. We started to lose our imagination, ability to trust, and our knowingness. We chose to live on Earth at this time and forgot how amazing we are. We lost our connection to our Souls and remembrance of who we are. We forgot our 5D selves but, you can't lose something that is already within you. You can cover it up all you want by piling on 3D ego over the years and blocking your potential but, eventually, your true self surfaces. It's why most in the spiritual guidance space help others to uncover their powers. We don't learn new things, we just start to unravel our greatness again.

The fire that burned within us as children was put out along the way. The smoke cleared, and our eyes stopped watering, but what was left? We end up carrying our aches, heartbreaks, pains, traumas, beliefs, and disbeliefs with us as we grow up, but do we really grow up?

There are so many delusions and illusions as to what Spiritual warfare is. Spiritual warfare is NOT outside of ourselves, it's within us. Fighting battles within is the only way to get to where we want to be. What if the "Devil" is inside of YOU? What if "negative" energy comes from YOU? You know, the deep darkness that you hold within you that goes against God and His Light. The trauma you ignore to process. All the pain and hurt you carry. All the injustice you have faced as a child and even as an adult.

Everyone that is walking this Earth at this time has CHOSEN to be here. We have chosen our roles, every situation we have and will experience. We have chosen to feel all these emotions, yes, even the hard ones. We have been well equipped before coming back to Earth with all the skills we need to be able to live our missions here. Some choose to exit early because they want to experience that. Some choose to live a long life to experience that.

Once I started telling people that I could connect to Spirit, the typical responses I received were:

"Oh that is so cool, I'm jealous!!"

"That's insane, it's the devil's work!"

"Can you read me right now and prove it?"

"How?"

I know why I chose to keep silent for so many years. I know why I felt like this "gift" would be a burden, a burning cross to carry, and that I would lose people along the way.

Never in my life did I say, "God give me this gift."

Never in my life did I "want" this.

Never in my life did I think this would be how I support my family.

But then I remembered that I DID CHOOSE this path like so many others.

Imagine that the 7.674 billion people on Earth right now already knew we would be facing all the things we are facing today. We have the capability to SIT STILL and awaken to our INNER KNOW-INGNESS.

In a world full of opportunities, we have set the most unbearable limitations on ourselves and society. We lump people into categories and end up missing out on the good. The possibilities of experiencing miracles become less and less. As a society, we've gotten so used to ostracizing anything and anyone that doesn't fit a specific perception of "normal." But, what is normal?

We categorize or label and start to miss the uniqueness of all of God's beautiful work. What would life look like if we took our blinders off? What if we stopped labeling everything and everyone? Take away the labels. Take away the human body. We are all souls of no color, gender, race, association, or affiliation. We are all of the same Universe. We are all innocent children walking this Earth.

Every day is a fight for me to keep my sanity. Every day is a fight to "shut it off or keep it on." I yell at God and put the blame on Him for believing in me so much when I don't always believe in myself. I battle my guide not to give me messages I don't want to deliver, but he knows I will and can handle it. They protect me from the hurt, but sometimes it's necessary for me to feel it.

There are days that I'm all in and others I want to quit. Deciphering messages and trying to share them with people when I know there's so much disbelief and fear around this is the most difficult part. I have fear and disbelief, too, but I also experience the joy, love, and happiness that gets delivered.

If everyone was created in the image and likeness of God, can women too channel the Holy Spirit? Did the Virgin Mary not hear God tell Her that She would birth the Son of God? That is called channeling. Why are men the only ones that can preach the Word of God?

I struggled with this for many years. I felt wrong for being able to receive the same messages that the priests were delivering to the masses. Why does a male that gets their calling from God have a superior status they can reach? They get to stand in front of millions of people to spread the Word of God, but yet, a woman who does it, she is seen as a witch. A woman who had the same gifts as a man got burnt at the stake because she too possessed the same gifts of men for years.

Men inherit their powers while in the womb of a female. As a medium, it was hard for me to accept my gifts. The same gifts that my Priest and even the Pope hold. Yet, they are seen as ones that are Holy and full of God. Meanwhile, I have been ridiculed and told what I'm doing is Evil by my own family members. I get it, how can little, boring me possess the same gifts of men who preach to the masses?

Should I too be burnt at the stake? Why do I not get a fancy house in Italy? Why do I not get a say in how people should "fear" God? This isn't just in the Roman Catholic Church. This is true for almost all religions. Some are quicker to an awakening of inclusion than others. But I'm not here to just talk about religion or women.

I'm blessed to have amazing family and friends that get it. They don't bat an eye when I tell them outrageous things, they just believe me. A husband that says, "ok, if that's what it is, then we will handle it." Friends that say, "I believe you and know it will be fine." They don't run away when I try to run away. They are my team. They are my people that lift me up when I'm at my lowest. I've faced some of the hardest criticism from people I love the most. In these times, I ask myself, what is the message here?

At any moment, we can be taught a lesson by someone smaller, younger, older, richer, poorer, smarter, or dumber. There are moments when the child teaches the parent, and the mentor becomes the mentee. There will come a day when we realize there is no such thing as labels. We have but ONE God/Source/Universe (however you practice) that is leading us.

When will you drop your armor? When will you LISTEN? Your soul is crying out for you to SEE and HEAR it. This is your "karma." This is why you are here. We are not here to fight each other. We are here to create unity in the biggest divide in human history. We are being called to STEP UP. We are being called to activate our beautiful souls that know love, peace, collaboration, and community. We are being called to look inward and heal the karmic debts our souls have lived.

*They are yearning to be set free.*

The ones that anger us the most are the ones that are teaching us the biggest lessons. As a society, we play the blame game, name call, and attack. There's a lot of misinformation out there in regards to energy, trauma, and healing. Energy is not good, bad, positive, or negative. It just IS. It is complementive. We are responsible for the energies we want to put out. Our karmic debts and traumas come back for lifetimes until we clear them or learn the lesson. Healing is not linear, there is no right or wrong way to heal. When we start to accept that it has nothing to do with them and everything to do with us, we reach clarity and enlightenment.

Until society can take ownership in how we charge or project our energy and trauma, we will continue to see destruction, war, hate, and pain. Do you believe that if we are willing to take a deep dive into ourselves to heal the wrongdoings of others and be responsible for our own decisions, the world could be a better place? We are not meant to react or respond to everything. We are simply here to observe and enjoy our lives. Everyone plays their roles, has their own timelines and responsibilities. Once we release the control of trying to fix others and look within, everything will change.

Give up the idea that spiritual warfare is something new. We have been fighting this fight for a long time. But, we are being called to change our strategy. We are not being weaponized with swords and armor. We are being equipped with self-love, unity, and Oneness.

We are here to walk this Earth in harmony, in unison with each other. Understanding each other's perspectives, even though they may be different from our own, is a step towards growth. We are here to spread God's love to all of "His" children. There should be no competition or superiority in this world. We are, and will all soon be, treated equal.

Warriors move differently. They intuitively plot their steps, take their time, conserve their energy; rest, recoup and march on. Warriors turn inward when the going gets tough. They know that they are the only ones responsible to fight the good fight within. They allow their soul the space and grace to grow up. They trust in a God that moves mountains, creates beauty in every way, loves, and protects us from things that are not meant for us. We were never burned at the stake. We were simply reborn time and time again.

*Arise from the ashes, the journey is not over, it's just beginning.*

Put down the phone. Shut off the TV. Reconnect with those who love you. Reconnect with God/Source/Universe. Reconnect with yourself. Our brains are so filled with illusions and delusions. Our hearts are pure, even with all the aches, pains, and messages for us.

If you could really hear a message from your soul, what would it be telling you? What would an in-depth clearing and cleansing of the different aspects of your life: mental, emotional, physical, and spiritual look like? What if you are able to uncover your authentic self?

What if I told you we already do this? We stare into mirrors all day. Everyone we cross paths with is a mirror to our soul. Remember illusions and delusions? This is it. We see the potential, best in, and love in others. We give people the benefit of doubt. We give them space and grace to grieve. We understand them and what they are going through. We offer help. But what we aren't realizing is that we are giving these people what we desire most: love and acceptance. We are so quick to serve others. The last person we feel called to serve is ourselves.

It's ass-backwards. We ARE beacons of light, but we can't be them if we continue to give our power to others. Warriors LEAD. They shine the brightest and don't dim their light. They call forward their sovereignty. They have honest conversations with themselves. I'll share one that I've had to work through.

I used to always focus on what other people needed. I believed everyone needed to change, but I would avoid the change myself. I wanted to control every situation in my life. Avoiding being hurt was what I tried to control the most. I would push people away before they could hurt me. I built a wall so strong and high around my heart that I missed out on so much love. As the years went on, it became unavoidable. I had to face the music.

I am grateful for every experience I've had in my life, good and bad. I used to ask myself, "What is my purpose? Why did I go through everything I've been through?"

And then it hit me. Everything I've dealt with has been so I can show people the Glory of God. How I've had everything taken away from me at different points in my life and then blessed with MORE in return. How I've had near-death experiences 4+ times where I knew God saved me. When I go through up levels (because they never end), I ask: what got me through it besides my family and friends?

*Amazing Grace.* I used to listen to it every day, and sometimes I forget, so I get little nudges to listen to it again and let the words work through me: *"Twas grace that taught my heart to fear and grace my fears relieved. How precious did that grace appear the hour I first believed."*

I remembered the first time I believed. I was about three years old, drowning in a pool, and saw the tunnel. My uncle pulled me out, but I have always remembered that moment. And now, 30+ years later, God is still saving me. On my lowest days, I sit and pray.

I remember one really hard moment when I felt called to put Holy Water on myself. I kept praying until my body stopped shaking. The cold feeling I had lifted off. My body got warm. I knew it was happening. I was being saved once again. Even in my darkest days, I've always had more than I'd ever need.

These up-levels start to ease up. You get used to them. Your awareness of self becomes clearer. Recently, I've been blessed with meeting members of my Soul Family. They aren't blood, but they are soul related. One even shares the exact same soul as me—some call it "Twin Flame" others "Divine Match." Connecting with him allowed me to see myself—the real me beneath all the ego.

It has been the best and worst months of my life. How could I meet someone thousands of miles away that I would connect so deeply with? Then I sit and think of all the decisions we've both had to make to get us to meet, and I'm amazed. All the miracles that had to happen for us to connect. All the failures, hurts, pains, and suffering we pushed through because we always knew there was something out there keeping us afloat. I remember when we first started to realize who we were, we both said, "You know I always felt like I was missing half of me."

Our souls knew. Our hearts lead us to each other. Love on the 5D plane is not what it is in 3D. The connection is MUCH deeper. We decided to meet in this timeline to become ONE. It doesn't mean that we are ONE together. Our souls are ready to be whole. We have spent many lifetimes clearing karma. We have learned many lessons along the way. We have chosen to heal the world from Original Sin and prove that forgiveness and love of self heals all, whether it's through one of us or both.

Big task, huh? When I was given this message, I freaked out. Why would I choose this? What is the purpose? It's not just with my "Twin Flame." It's been with every soul I've encountered along the way to heal myself. It's also not just about me, I'm not that important.

BETRAYAL LEADS TO FORGIVENESS. God forgave Adam and Eve, but it was their human ego that did not allow themselves to accept His forgiveness. They have spent YEARS within all of us trying to heal. The only way we are able to help them attain freedom is by freeing ourselves. We are making a movement from 3D to 5D. Self-love and acceptance are what's needed most.

When you're heading towards self-mastery and Divinity, you are able to see outside of yourself. How does Divinity look? A little like this:

Being worthy because you breathe.

Being beautiful because you believe you are.

Being loved because you love yourself.

Being a warrior because nothing has killed you yet.

*Divine Feminine power is a birthright.* It's worthiness, beauty, love, and warrior strength.

Being successful because you're not attached to the outcome.

Being intuitive because you listen to your own wisdom.

Being strong because you are present and humble.

Being grounded because you are in touch with your emotions.

*Divine Masculine power is a birthright.* It's intuitive, strategic, present, grounded, and humbled.

Everyone has both. It is not gender specific. CLAIM IT. It's a thought process. Stay present and aligned. Watch yourself jump. Divine Unison is being whole with yourself and God. That is THE END GAME.

## About the Author

### SIERRA GRANA

Sierra Grana is a Soul Gratifying Coach, Medium and Speaker who guides leaders, pioneers and generational curse breakers through their darkest moments to bring them towards their light.

Before starting her coaching career, Sierra was a Licensed Massage Therapist and held upper management positions over a 12 year span. After a successful but stressful career, Sierra shifted into what ignited her Soul: helping people live in the moment. With an undeniable Divine Aura, she has become the go to person for others who have lost their way. Sierra channels Spirit to help create authenticity, freedom, love, and joy with ease.

Sierra is a devoted wife and mother who enjoys spending time with her family, cooking, traveling and sports. She is available for transformational coaching and healing retreats in Egypt.

Email: sierragranacoaching@gmail.com
Website: https://www.sierragrana.com/
Facebook Page : https://www.facebook.com/sierragranacoaching/
Instagram & Clubhouse: @sierragranacoaching

FIFTEEN

# Nisha Ukani Velani

## HARNESSING THE POWER OF THE AKASHIC REALM AS A DIVINE CHANNEL OF GOD

What is it you think you know about yourself, others, the world?

That things need to be a certain way in order to 'achieve' success?

That people need to behave in a certain way to be worthy of respect and love?

That this life is a series of obstacles that we just need to 'get through'?

Are you on autopilot because of these beliefs?

Have you been allowing the conditions, wounding, and trauma of this lifetime, past life times, parallel lifetimes and, ancestral coding to drive the vessel of your life? Could this be your driving force without your knowledge or awareness?

So many of us walk around like zombies. Tethered to our ego identities, the identities that we build in the mind and body from what influences us externally.

But the soul knows differently.

The soul is here for EVERYTHING divine.

I look around and I see so many people living this way—who don't even realise they are doing so. I was one of them.

Walking around like a robot, feeling that everything was happening TO me. Living a double life steeped in shoulds, woulds, and coulds.

But the truth is, my soul knew there was more for me. There is a reason why I am here at this time in the evolution of the planet.

My magic is needed. As is yours.

I walked myself through the internal split of being a good girl and wanting to be a rebel, mostly coming from ego. Slowly coming back to my soul and realising that I am whole. And this is what so many of us NEED.

I knew I was destined for more. I spent many years working in the not for profit and charity sector trying to figure out my innate NEED to help people.

But I never felt I was good at the work. I never felt fully satisfied. I never felt fully at peace.

We are taught that these concepts, such as being satisfied through our work and being at peace in life, are unattainable and far reaching—they will never be available to us and don't belong in our reality.

That this world is purely to survive through.

This world is purely to struggle to search for joy, love and peace.

Being a first generation Indian in Great Britain, has meant that the lived experience of much of my family and community has been of trying to navigate intense times, survival, scarcity, lack, and fear. This travels in our DNA. The pain of ancestors in the earth timeline of persecution, the stripping of identity and wealth.

This combined with many past lives as a medicine woman and having been murdered countless times for my innate power and gifts, created a melting pot in my shadow body. A body full of deep-seated pain and struggle, much of which isn't even 'mine'. Most of us experience this and it is presented as repeated patterns (shadow coding) that mean we function on autopilot, perpetuating patterns and behaviours that no longer serve us.

We are all unique, we are all magic. We are all psychic. But we all have layers of shadow coding to detangle. To peel back, to learn from and shift.

And it's no coincidence that my biggest challenge, around being seen and heard, made itself present in this lifetime. I have been persecuted many times for this. I have seen lifetimes hanging in nooses, being drowned, and being burnt. But also, many lifetimes as a wise guide, healer, mentor, and soul activator.

One lifetime was spent with a sorcerer who betrayed me for my power as a witch, slitting my throat because of his power hunger. Other lifetimes were spent rotting in dungeons chained up. I've also spent a life supporting women fleeing from persecution and being murdered for it. Often it can sound fantastical, but these experiences carry coding that create energetic binding (shadow) which can affect us in this human experience. Weighing us down in many areas including safety in our bodies, personal power, and pleasure.

We also make vows and agreements with others and ourselves which need to be renounced. I had a vow around annihilating evil, which was made from ego, and had created many patterned behaviours around being surrounded and calling in dark experiences.

Our DNA can also carry curses which need to be broken. These can also create patterned behaviours and can cause someone to unwillingly call in repeated experiences such as premature deaths, illness and recurring abuse.

The many layers of active shadow you hold in the body are the cause of dormant layer of soul power, that is waiting to be unleashed.

We are here to live our deepest expression of our souls. To explore every part of it and bring it into 3D reality. To fulfil all our true heart desires from love and the divine. The task is to decipher what is ego/shadow. And what is pure desire.

This is where my work in the Akashic realm comes in. I work as a conduit for the divine to perform deep clearings and healings with precision, because it is what I am guided to do by God.

This is why the work I have done with clients is mind blowing and life altering and propels them on their highest timeline.

To hold such gifts, we must lead from our hearts, to stay constantly within integrity and to be able to heal shadow and put ego aside— meaning seeing and honouring who we are at a soul level. It takes mastery and precision. And is a natural gift for me. I don't have to think about what I am doing, because it is my soul doing the 'work'. Most of the healing I perform doesn't have labels. It's connection to the divine is pure and therefore the work I do is untainted.

The souls that are guided to work with me are the ones who are here to lead the earth into the next stage of ascension at this crucial time. To work in the highest timeline for themselves and the collective. To bring in the new, to honor ancient wisdom and to be supporting the new communities of the future. They are soul warriors and they have been working towards this for eons, just like I have.

Ancient wisdom needs to be cracked open via the heart, and the body needs to be a clear channel for the true potency of pure divinity to do its work.

This means that shadow must be cleared, and ego must be witnessed, embraced, and transcended.

This is why my work is a powerful tool. I see, feel, know (even when ego screams I am not) that I am a vessel for Gods work.

So I ask these questions:

What is your soul asking of you right now?

Is it asking that you delve deeper into awareness and exploration of self?

Is it yearning and longing to be seen, heard and felt?

Is it needing to break free from the cage it has been imprisoned in?

It is imperative at this time that you listen to your soul.

Carrying down a path of ignoring it means you walk a path of shaky foundations and disconnection from what is TRULY happening, and what the divine desires you to KNOW and BE.

So much magic awaits you, when you listen to your soul.

Everything you desire to be able to do is available to you. It was planted in your heart for a reason by God.

When I initially attempted to access the Akashic realm, via the records I was unsuccessful. My body was unable to hold the frequency of them for long. I had ascension symptoms because my body was full of toxicity, anxiety, depression, and a negative mindset. My body was operating at shadow frequency.

This was a wake-up call to start looking at the shadow that was sitting in my body. What I mean by shadow is, energetic 'blocks' that inhibit the natural flow of life force energy. I had stagnant energy that needed to be shifted so that I could reawaken my life force energy. I know that if I hadn't chosen to, the result would have been the manifestation of serious illness in my body.

God was showing me all the things that needed to be shifted in order for me to truly wake up—to begin understanding my purpose in this lifetime.

The thing with 'waking up' for most, is that it doesn't look like a slap in the face and a massive download about exactly what you are here to do. It actually looks like an exquisite unfurling of the soul, a process of clues given that you must follow using your most divine tool; intuition.

This is the key to opening your psychic gifts.

But back to my story :)

I started down a path of deep awakening, it wasn't smooth—it rarely is. For a period of time I put aside accessing the records because I was scared. But I was awake enough to see what the divine was laying in my path—healers, mentors, and coaches for me to follow. Even though I was deeply shrouded in shadow and in a 9-5 job that was literally killing my soul, I kept on exploring, investing and holding onto the small flame of faith that was alight inside.

I know many of us come close to giving up. That was me many times. At some points it felt too excruciating to continue, I was feeling so lost in the 'should' of what I was conditioned to be and forgetting who I really was. I was deeply unhappy and moving through days being unkind to myself.

Even through this I knew that I had to keep going. To keep taking steps forward even though I couldn't see the destination. Many of us have this voice, but so many choose not listen and do not dig deep for the courage to follow it. Bravery is key if we want to truly know ourselves.

There are steps in our lives we must take, like divine sign posts, which unlock the next level of the 'game'. Making bold choices and moves which allow us to expand our energetic field to hold more of the incredible blessings that are available to us.

It isn't all doom and gloom. We are here to create ALL that we desire. We have just forgotten who we are.

We are fighting many battles on many levels, but we must start with the self and clearing the shadow ( past, current and ancestral - conditioning, wounding trauma ) that is keeping us small. We understand that ego is trying to keep us safe, but how do we move past the shackles of it?

The Akashic realm has allowed me to break generational and ancestral curses in order to set souls free. There is darkness over time that has infiltrated layers of our cells and resides in our physical being and the layers of auric field.

My gifts mean that I am able to hear the divine in seeing where these are hidden in our fields and clear them. This in turn makes space for new DNA activations and also allows space for other suppressed layers to be revealed and to be cleared.

There is so much our body is hiding or that we neglect to feel, see and understand. It is a key part in healing the soul. We often think our physical symptoms are a result of what we eat, which is true to a certain extent. But what we hold in our cells is also key.

We can hold shadow coding in our cells; deep heavy emotions such as shame and guilt. Our natural divine body is light, clean, and pure.

Clearing shadow raises your energetic baseline frequency where you can become a resonant match for the frequencies of joy and love. Our home frequency is where the soul flourishes. Although we will still experience the spectrum of emotion as humans, this is what we are here to experience—Both/And. Meaning whilst you still feel, you are no longer living in the depths of weight in your being.

The shadow often dictates how we judge ourselves, how unkindly we speak to ourselves, and how we perceive how others see us. It dictates our filter in how we see the world.

We hold so much pain in our bodies, especially as women, a big part of my work is around the womb and supporting women to realise and heal violations that may have occurred in this lifetime but also past lives and generationally.

The womb space is so sacred, and we have lost the wisdom to pay reverence to it. It is a portal to life and creativity. It has been strangled and suppressed for too long.

In clearing layers and layers of dead stagnant energy, we can bring in space for NEW divine light. The key to this is play and pleasure and deep satisfaction of the body and soul.

The Akashic realm allows us to clear and bring in new codes and activate those that are lying dormant in our DNA. This is why many of my clients experience deep activation from being in my field. Their psychic gifts are cracked open, and their bodies are filled with light coding. It is the most joyous part of my work, as I can see the activation taking place within the body and field.

As my work is divinely guided, I only clear, heal, and activate what is for the highest good and timeline for them. And they are never given more than they are available for. I am not here to work from ego and to push my clients beyond what is nourishing for them in the moment.

The work is so potent that they will continue to experience activations and healing long after we work together. Deeper awareness, deeper transformation, and deeper gifts to share with the world.

We must not forget the importance of how our bodies work through the chakra system and the flow of energy and how alive it is. Reactivating is priority in order to SEE clearly.

This work is true alchemy through the power of the divine. It is not learned, it just is. It is always channelled, and always unique to the soul. Always ever evolving—deepening. It is exactly what is needed at exactly the right time. This is why it is incredibly precise and divine in nature. It is ancient wisdom.

And so, I'll ask you some further questions:

In what part of your life do you feel like you 'should' be doing things a certain way? Where do you follow that voice that is shrouded in fear? The voice that doesn't feel good, but you go along with anyway, hand in hand feeling like you are supported, when in fact you are traveling further away from your power.

Where in life do you feel small and attacked? Allowing others to dictate how you feel about yourself and/or your surroundings?

Where in life are you not permitting yourself the things you know you truly desire to experience?

Are you imitating life because that's what you 'see' around you?

Or are you tapped into the divine and the infinite possibilities of what is available to you?

Expression of self comes in many forms, through play, pleasure, art, creativity. What is it that sets your soul on fire? I recently re-discovered my love for art and now create art portals infused with upgrade energy specifically for a soul. It's so potent, fun and magical.

For my clients, it is the deep feeling of yearning that brings them to me. They step into another level of bravery because they know they can no longer ignore the call. Their lives are not fulfilled. They may be making great money, but they feel disconnected from others. Discontent and not knowing fully why. They are conscious and listen to the nudges of their soul. They KNOW they must go deeper to ascend higher.

There are certain types of bonds and experiences that our souls have contracted to transcend, heal, and clear and this wisdom is in your Akashic records. You may have a certain person who you are struggling to connect with or walk away from. There may be vows or curses connected to them.

Many of my clients take vows which they are unaware of, and this dictates a massive pattern throughout multiple lifetimes.

For example, a beautiful client of mine was experiencing repetition in giving away her power to a certain type of man—aggressive controlling. We discovered a vow that had been made with an entity in a past life that meant this pattern reappeared for her in the most painful current experiences. In breaking this vow, we removed a massive layer of darkness that has allowed a break in the pattern and clarity around how to move forward in this lifetime.

The work I do with clients is magic and true alchemy. Not many have the innate skill and wisdom to see through the layers and pinpoint the source. Not many are able to hone in and clear, with purity, that which is no longer serving them.

192

It is time to purge the invasion of our souls and move forward in light and power and bring in all that we desire. Are you with me?

Allow whatever needs to flow out of you come, don't shut down when an idea springs to mind, often the first thought is the clue.

Some of us need more time to respond to things—that's ok too. There is beauty in learning about ourselves. We are in such a hurry to get to the outcome that we often forget to see the incredible expansion in learning about ourselves, wooing ourselves, and falling in love with ourselves.

### Start here and the rest follows.

Letting go of the FOMO and the idea of being left out, of not being invited to things, or what people think of you.

If someone forgets your birthday, not holding it against them. And loving yourself enough if they do, so it doesn't matter.

Not getting caught up in the way people 'should' behave. And expecting things to be a certain way, from fear.

We don't even realise we are making decisions based on fear. At any moment we can make a choice to see things a different way. And give ourselves compassion if we are sad, hurt, or angry, but know that these do not run the show. That you can take an action from a place of an expanded vibration which is in tune with the real Self.

It is constantly choosing who you desire to be, whilst not ignoring all the human experience is offering to show you.

We must be more nuanced and sophisticated in understanding the multilevel healing that needs to take place. Sometimes it is not a matter of one plus one equals two. Healing is not linear. True alchemy is not linear. And the Akashic Realm does not work in a linear way. The Divine does not work in a linear way.

It doesn't matter what others think. You must stay true to your soul. Work through the layers of conditioning that dictates that you must do certain things for other people. That you must be seen in a certain way. That to behave in the right way is the right thing. Release the self-inflicted pressure. Release yourself from the shackles.

This double life you lead is splitting you in two. Soul wants you to come back to wholeness. It desires you to be ALL that you are. To bring in your gifts and land them in this space and time to help others to do the same. We are all here supporting each other through pure community. This is what the new earth will be.

You are the key to your life. What do you choose? To dance and play through life or see it as an endless set of struggles. Perception is everything and by clearing the heaviness and shadow from your field you allow your soul voice to run the show of your life. To call in the magical experiences and to navigate the highs and the lows with grace and compassion for yourself and others.

Step INTO who you truly are—expansion is always calling—but are you listening? Drop the wall—allow it all in. Soul is calling you home, are you brave enough to walk the path there?

## About the Author

### NISHA UKANI VELANI

Nisha Ukani Velani is a deep level, multi-dimensional, energy healer, an intuitive life coach, mentor, guide and modern day mage.

Through harnessing the power of the Akashic realm and as a channel for the divine she guides souls to heal, clear and transmute shadow so they can bring their pure desires to life. As a soul code activator, Nisha awakens dormant DNA to deepen soul connection and create massive impact in all areas of life. Utilising skills in psychic surgery she also helps conscious leaders uncover their shadow bodies and lives, shedding what no longer serves them and bridging the gap between soul desires and embracing the human experience.

Nisha lives in London, U.K with her husband, and is motivated by her mission of inspiring other souls to rise in love, through the divine. She loves travelling the world, being by the sea, dancing and painting. She is a massive Potterhead and is still searching for the perfect broomstick that will allow her to play Quidditch.

Email: nishaukanivelani@gmail.com
Website: https://www.nishaukanivelani.com/
Facebook: https://www.facebook.com/nisha.ukani.1/
Instagram: https://www.instagram.com/nisha_velani/
Clubhouse: https://www.clubhouse.com/@nishavelani

SIXTEEN

# Dayla Del Toro

## TRUST YOUR TIMELINE

To be able to jump from this Earthly experience to any other, you have to first acknowledge that you are chosen to be here. It is not always something a person can believe about themselves. But this one realization can free your soul, like a key to the doors of interdimensionality.

It took me 25 years of feeling out of place to truly do a deep dive into what it takes to be grounded. It may feel unimportant to be grounded on this Earth, but the truth is, to be connected to your soul's journey, you have to understand why your soul chose to be here at this time and at this place.

There is a prolonged awkwardness of not feeling at home in your body. What is interesting about the journey to beyond the veil of this reality, is we have to achieve a comfort in our skin here. Not just in our bodies, but in the time and place that we are put upon this Earth. One of the things that I encounter in Past Life Regression Therapy is that before we begin, during the consultation phase and pre-work, my clients often express that a piece of their curiosity of past lives revolves around not feeling at home in this life. They wish to be in a different time or place, a different body, a different gender, many things come up. While this is completely normal to the human experience, an acceptance of your soul's journey begins by digging in and grounding yourself in the why of "Why did my soul choose here and now for me? What can I learn here?"

It's almost impossible to deny there are beings beyond this realm with all the scientific research that has come out on this topic. Researchers from The Blue Brain Project out of Switzerland realized our own brain can create neuron structures in up to 11 dimensions. When we look at what this means on and off Earth, and the communion that we can have with beings of these dimensions, we can feel more at home knowing that our soul chose to be presented in this dimension of emotional connectivity, the 3rd dimension. We use and are aware of only eight percent of our brain. Three percent of this is used for autonomic functions, like breathing. So the ninety-two percent of functions we are unaware of are constantly working, building, creating and connecting to dimensions beyond our conscious awareness.

There is something beautiful about realizing the immense space taken up by our bodies, at the same time that we humans are infinitesimally small compared to the Earth we reside on. In a state of meditation, and sometimes in the brain waves between awake and asleep, some of us have this realization. Think of the falling dreams that we can all relate to, where you're almost asleep and your brain suddenly envisions falling and bursts you into alertness. In that same brain wave state, many of us have a similar dream scare, where we shrink down to a quantum or cellular size, and suddenly are larger than the whole galaxy. It can be comforting or terrifying, depending on the chemicals being released by your brain. Using this visualization is one of the ways we can both ground ourselves into the heart of residing in both our soul state and also go beyond the realms of this Earth and connect to the interdimensionality of being.

One of the most powerful ways that I help people realize their DNA is active in many dimensions at the same time, is through a visualization of yourself as one cell body, and then becoming a being of light beyond measurable size. We do this together in order to feel ourselves beyond duality, beyond separation of your soul body, my soul body, and your neighbor's soul body. Because while you are you, here in this time and this place, you are also only a fraction of you, here in this time and place. There are pieces of you living what we think of as "past lives," but these lives are all lived simultaneously, and they are both lived and remembered simultaneously beyond the constraints of spacetime. Your mind exists in this body, accessing a fraction of it's consciousness, while it's connections through the dimensions link your mind to all your bodies beyond this world. When we sit together in a past life regression session, the fractions of you as you think you are, and the fraction of me here with you, are both pieces of a bigger soul body that is of the same life and the same resonance through time and space. We link to your memories across all these lives in all the bodies you exist in. We, and all beings here on Earth, can be considered cells with different functions on a larger Earth body. Just like a blood cell and a brain cell have different functions in our body, but live their cell life, so too could you  serve different functions on the larger Earth body but together with other humans create a functioning world.

We ground ourselves to serve not only our purpose, but the purpose of Earth's survival so that in our life and our life on this planet we serve the purpose of thriving. We can ask our universal energy flow, how is it that we all can thrive here? How am I being supported to thrive in my body, on this planet, and in the greatness of the universe?

During the Random Number Generator Project study done by Princeton University, scientists set up an experiment in order to test if the presence of life and consciousness can bend the very reality that surrounds it. They set up a light on an active arm in the center of the ceiling in a square room. When the room was empty, they began the random number generator on the moving arm so it would aim at one of the four corners randomly over a set length of time. In both short lengths of time and longer intervals, all four corners had an equal number of times the light would randomly aim at each corner of the room.

The next part of the study is where it gets interesting. When they introduced a living being into the room, in this case a plant, where light was necessary for the plant to survive, the random number arm was pulled more times to shine in whatever position the plant was in. They tested short intervals of time, long intervals of time, moving the plant to different areas of the room, and no matter what they changed, the living nature of the plant altered the physical reality so the plant had better odds to survive.

When we look at life outside of these studied contexts, we see that nature creates situations where living beings can either be designed with the best odds for survival or they can be given in enough quantity that they have the most chances for survival (quality DNA or quantity DNA). The nature of the universe wants the most possible thriving experiences for beings here on Earth. At a cellular level, our bodies want our cells to survive and thrive. At a planetary level, the Earth has this innate ability to balance itself to homeostasis.

You are not meant to struggle. You are not meant to perish. You are here to align with the will of creation and a conscious resonance with your ability to thrive. You are here to realize that your consciousness bends reality to match you and creates the systems that allows you the light of life. You are not an unconscious, unliving piece of matter in a dark room. You are a living, light of life seeking being that can shift reality around you to thrive.

One of the biggest pieces to our human and interdimensional existence is our connectivity. Many clients, when they arrive for past life regression sessions, are looking for evidence of the connections they have in this life existing beyond time in other lives. This could be their parents, a friend, a spouse, their children, or anyone that they feel deeply connected to that they can search for recognition in other lives. So much of the flow of our emotional state depends on this interconnectedness and the balance between the emotional states of others. This is part of our lesson and part of our experience.

Before we are born, we are connected to the soul guides and fragments of our being that lead us here to be in this place at this time. We are connected to our mother in the womb, and the people that surround our mother as we prepare for our time of true being. This begins our web of connectivity and experience. When, or if, these connections falter, fail, or seem to end in this life, that does not mean that they end in all the lives. Time is indifferent to the journey of connectivity we are meant to experience with aligned souls. In one life, you may have a sibling for a number of years, but in another life, the same soul is your spouse for a time, or simply a short formative experience. When one fraction of the same soul dies in one life, they can still be alive in other lives along their timeline. Because these timelines are nonlinear, when you call upon someone you've lost in this life you are experiencing, you may receive recognition from multiple fragments of their souls in the spiritual reality. They are as close to you in all times as it would be to hold your own hand. Your fragments experiencing their life timelines are as close to you as both timelines closing your eyes at the same time.

This is why many times in our lives we experience sensations like deja vu. This is also why in dreams we may align with our "past" and "future" lives and see things that seem like premonitions or memories that are recognized as real. We can mourn the loss of a connection because we feel, deeply, that they are lost forever, when in reality, they are forever connected in our web of experience and will continue to show themselves. We are, all of us, connected in multiple realities of existence at once. Our most divine selves, what people on this Earth would define as a 9th or 11th dimensional being, are as simultaneous as your life and my life playing out upon the 3rd dimension. The other dimensions are existing and accessible in our minds, as we create synapses in all of these dimensions. But we have to be in a specific brain wave- length to see the layers and access the realities that live there. We have to exist in the in-between of awake and asleep to navigate this area.

The historical gift of hypnotic and trance states is where ancient shamans and us, in the modern era, can coexist and navigate these areas of space time. Hypnosis and trance, which can be used synonymously, predate written history. When we study ancient civilizations, we also see that whole communities would enter this state together and as one mind, to access and decipher their place, purpose, and meaning here on this Earth. With or without the use of guiding substances (as many communities used ceremonial psychedelics to reach deeper states of trance), the mind can reach the information.

The mind creates and exists in all the dimensions at once, and when you can ground in to being designed to be here, let go of emotion and expectation, and shine the light of being into the cellular world that exists in matter, while also diving into the darkness of the empty spaces between your cells, you are navigating within yourself the vastness of the real universe.

When I activate this power of navigation within people, I show them the DNA that exists within them in the now, while also giving them the missing DNA structures that are no longer visible to us in the 3rd dimension. Our soul's DNA has been fractured, and this is what gives us the ability to exist and experience in multiple realities at once. But in this fractioning, there is also an erasure, a mass forgetting. It is the forgetting that gives us the ability to have an unbiased, new experience in the 3rd dimension. Which is why when we are in the life between lives, our soul guides decide if we will go into our new womb space with a shadow of memory of a life before. Many children are able to remember small pieces of the before, but over time, their brains are wiped of these shadows for a more naive and new experience.

Through the hypnotic experience, grounding, and ascension, we are gifted the ability to see our DNA as a whole. Of the humans that are here on this Earth, the scientific study of the human genome has only an estimated 40 million sequences that match amongst us. However, there are over 300 million sequences that do not match ancestral samples. Where does this mysterious DNA come from? How did these DNA structures that completely overshadow our human ancestry come to be in our 3rd dimensional experience?

These DNA codes are gifts, and they are here to help us define our place not just on this Earth, but in the whole of the Universe. These codes are here to give us the bigger picture of ancestry and interdimensionality that we have lost , across wars and annihilated ancient cities and civilizations that the greater political and social agenda would manipulate and erase to have us forget.

We cannot forget our DNA records, as they exist within us to have and to hold for all of reality. By going within, by accessing the states of our brain that exist in the in between, we can always find the information that our greater soul would have us remember. One of the greatest gifts we can give ourselves is opening this state of mind and of being alongside others. When we go into the community trance states, we are not only unlocking our DNA, but we are connecting the same soul parts of our DNA that we share with our fellow human. What's beautiful about this Earth, and the way that other animals have evolved here, we have and can access these states across multiple species. The more we study mammals and the greater whole of communication, we realize that animal language surpasses what we believed it did before. Attribute this belief to an egocentric view of the world, that hindered our ability to recognize that animals have been here evolving alongside us, and have actually been trying to communicate with us for millenia. Even animals we look at with completely different brains and brain structures, from octopi to elephant, to bird to orangutan, all have the ability to understand and communicate. Thus, we have to be open and receptive to their desire to connect. Through this connectivity we define our place, our purpose, and our meaning.

What exactly is it that crosses the veil of all realities? What is it that pulls us in these connections, beyond time, beyond space, and beyond experience?

You can look at it scientifically or spiritually, the answer is love. The one thing that brings us through all, that mysteriously heals, that creates whole belief systems, that redefines the nature of existence, that thing is love. We study the frequency of love, of positive belief, and of aligning ourselves with what creates our reality. The the thing that has more power than anything is the frequency of love. It can be explained simply like this— if you were in a massive realm with no stars, no moon, no positivity, no love, the absence of everything, and some being came into that presence with nothing else to add, or only darkness or what we see as negative space, it would not get darker. It couldn't. There is only the empty. But if even one being came into that space with a single light, ready to connect, ready to ignite more lights, ready to spark love, belief, inspiration in others, not only would you be able to see that being and the beings surrounding and connecting that being, but you would also see how much intensity and inertia they ignited in others. In this way, the introspection of a soul and exploration of who you are and what your purpose is here and finding love within yourself, you can then see and have compassion and empathy for others in all states and dimensions.

By being love, you spread love. By seeing love, you create love. By being within yourself what you wish to create, so too does the universe create with you. Love isn't a plan, or a representation of perfection. It is a state of choice. It is the conscious creation of a thriving soul. It isn't about a feeling of safety or of sureness, it is about realizing that there isn't a chase for happiness or perfection, it is about feeling the connection, the oneness, the whole.

# About the Author

## DAYLA DEL TORO

Dayla Del Toro is a Licensed Provider of Neuro-Linguistic Programing or NLP, Hypnotherapy, and Past Life Regression therapy. In September 2020, she opened Bask Healing to serve people with neurodivergence, PTSD and C-PTSD, addicts of all kinds, and those with disordered eating as an ally and an integrative coach. She offers 1-on-1 and educational courses as well as hands-on healing therapies. In 2021, while pregnant with her son, she added Hypnotic Birth to her practice, trained by The Mongan Hypnobirthing Institute.

Bask Healing offers healing retreats and online intensives for more in depth healing work, breaking down chronic habits, and re-aligning the self with it's purpose. She and her family live in Spain, spreading the light of soul-aligned action with others and helping people realize their purpose.

Dayla has openings in her intensives year round, if you'd like to explore them or contact her, browse baskhealing.com or thedayla. baskhealing@gmail.com

# SEVENTEEN

# Leeann Kime

## HOW MY SPIRIT TEAM HELPED ME THROUGH...

My very bad long-suffering marriage was coming to an end, and I knew I had to leave for the safety and future development of my beautiful daughter and myself.

The time to leave had been an agonizing decision for over seven years, and I knew that I would have to wait until my daughter was older, could speak her own mind, and was able to make decisions for herself. If I did not do this, I would have had even more difficulty in caring for her and keeping her safe.

I found the time to leave was a completely guided time from my spirit team and I had to move quickly. The time was two days before Christmas. When I left, not a lot of people knew there were problems with my marriage, or that I was leaving a volatile situation. I left with my daughter and a huge sense of relief.

We had very little money, only about $500 in savings and no furniture. We did not even have a bed to sleep in. We had minimal personal possessions and my daughter's father had made it very clear that we would not receive his support in any way. He made it as difficult as possible for us to leave.

He assisted in no way with child support until after a lengthy process was put in place where he was required by law to make payments. He also managed to divert some of his income so that he paid a minimal amount of child support. He would stalk us at the shopping centers. He would park his car outside our house, and I would have to call the police to have him removed.

I worked three part time jobs and did whatever I could to support myself and my daughter. We received some help from my mum which was a blessing.

Not long after we left, I became unwell. I had some tests done and it was discovered that I had a raised level of prolactin in my blood test. As I was not pregnant or lactating, I was sent for an MRI scan, and it revealed that I had a growth in my head. I was insanely scared as I had no money, I was working three part time casual jobs, and I had my daughter to support. WHAT DO I DO WITH THIS NEWS?? I was so scared for my future and for the future of my daughter.

With years of energy training and having built a deep connection with my spirit team, I was guided to sit and meditate about my health and how to heal. During meditation, I was shown a very clear movie and received messages from my spirit team. It was such a blessing and relief that I had such a close connection with my spirit team, especially at this time of receiving such potentially catastrophic news of the growth in my head. I trusted that my spirit team would assist and guide me once again.

I had been fully assisted and guided by my spirit team previously when I lost my baby twins at 22 weeks into the pregnancy. I delivered my twin boys prematurely and I knew that they would pass away shortly after their birth. Prior to giving birth, I was shown by my spirit team what would occur and the total experience prior to the birth, during the birth, and post the birth, which assisted me through the gift and loss of new life.

I was completely assisted and guided at both a deep soul level and physical level by my spirit team. As a result of this complete guidance, support, and assistance of my spirit team, I was helped through the process of the death of my twin boys, milk leaking every time I walked for days after their birth, the funeral and burial, and going back to work and having to answer all the questions from colleagues and clients. I was also guided, supported and assisted by my spirit team to work through the grief process without becoming a total wreck. My spirit team guided me to find the gift that is present in grief and there is truly a big gift in grief.

At the burial of my twin boys, my spirit team showed me there is a beautiful gift in each moment. When the little coffin of my twin boys was lowered into the ground, two butterflies flew over the top of the grave and around the surrounding area. The two butterflies continued to fly around in unison and make their presence known for about 15 minutes. I knew my spirit team was with me and my twin boys at that time. It was truly a beautiful sight and experience.

Years later when I was shown the clear movie and received messages from my spirit team, I knew that I needed to wholeheartedly follow and trust in what I was shown. I was shown the exact steps to follow to heal. I was also shown that I would have a scan to show the growth in my head and a subsequent scan to show that it has disappeared.

For many months, I followed the exact steps that I was shown, I was guided every day in meditation, and I received healing from my spirit team. When the day arrived to have the subsequent scan, the growth in my head was GONE!

Prior to healing, I was again shown by my spirit team what would occur and the total experience of being shown the exact steps to follow to heal assisted me through my healing journey. It was truly an amazing healing experience to have undergone with my spirit team, just as much as my experience of losing my baby twins was with their guidance and support.

In the years that followed and up to this point in time, I am continually mentored, guided, supported, and taught many things by my spirit team. My spirit team are continually assisting me through my own life and they also teach me how to assist others in the development of soul connection and how to live a life that is fully soul connected and full of hearts desire.

My life is full of love and soul connection as a result of partnering my life with my spirit team. There is never a day that goes by without being in deep connection with them.

It is my wish that you too may feel the love, support, and guidance of amazing spirit team connection.

Sending you love, Leeann

## About the Author

### LEEANN KIME

As an experienced coach, Leeann has mentored women into embodying their feminine presence for 30 years through yoga, meditation, Ayurveda, Medical Intuition and the Art of Feminine Presence. Leeann has decades of psychic partnership with Spirit Mentors, and with their insights and healing, she guides clients to experience l joy and fulfillment in life.

Leeann works with clients at a deep soul level to facilitate change in re-patterning and rewire energy fields. Together with the Spirit Mentors, Leeann creates change gently, lovingly and powerfully, impacting deep internal shifts that create core energetic reconstruction of old soul debris, negative patterning and outdated energetic loops. Leeann encourages all to live life with soul connection and expression.

Website: https://leeannkime.wixsite.com/landingpage

Facebook: https://www.facebook.com/Heartful-Soul-Matters-103968315433902

# EIGHTEEN

## YuSon Shin

### RISING ABOVE STRUGGLES UNIQUE TO A SOUL WARRIOR TO SHINE

The lives of soul warriors, aka light workers, can appear glamourous, miracle-filled, and magical—and they often are. The stereotype and social media accounts of these light workers often highlight only the good parts and create an illusion of a perfect, magical life, as if their gifts just dropped into their lap. However, the life-long struggles faced by these individuals, usually over many years, to reach the point where their lives finally do appear magical to the outside world are quite often not readily acknowledged.

As a healer, medium, and intuitive, I can absolutely attest to the magic of working in the light and allowing Source, angels, guides, and my inner GPS to steer me in the right direction. I have asked for and experienced my master guide telling me his name in a deep, booming voice outside of my head. As a medium, I have seen signs left by people in spirit for those who remain in the physical body. I have seen baby spirits come forward to greet their future parents. Angels have lovingly guided me to work with them even though I did not know anything about them before they revealed themselves, such as during my Sedona trip a few years ago when Archangel Ariel introduced herself to me as my new primary archangel working with me going forward (replacing Archangel Michael). As a medical medium, I sometimes receive names of illnesses and diseases that I am not familiar with during sessions with clients and find out later that my client learns from their doctor the diagnosis is the same. I am a former logic-based, analytical, and rational real estate paralegal, so these feel like little miracles to me. Ironically, I now live half my waking life in the mysterious, unexplainable world of healing and spirits.

As amazing as evidence like that often is, the path of a light warrior is also riddled with struggles, doubt, loneliness, lack of support, and validation as we see and feel what others cannot and often do not believe is "real." Newly activated light warriors are the most vulnerable to these downsides because they don't yet have the years of repeated validations that these things "cannot just be a coincidence" and the supportive social networks comprised of other light workers to support them and guide them through their initial confusion, excitement, and sometimes fear. Even seasoned soul warriors doubt their abilities and feel disheartened enough to consider giving up or disillusioned enough to believe that devoting so much time and effort to working in the light isn't their calling after all. It takes years of the Universe giving us validation before we trust ourselves and understand what we are seeing with our third eye and feeling in our gut. Our path is often lonely and may not be validated until reviewed in hindsight.

Some are born with this calling to be a soul warrior, and others are awakened to answer this call to be of service at some point in their life. By answering this call, we have agreed to enlist in the war of light versus dark. We have volunteered to help transmute darkness into light. We have committed to living life lit up from our soul and to help show others the way. Light workers choose to be radiant and hold light and love like light sabers in each hand to cut a path for others. We are trailblazers who create paths in our own unique ways, both big and small, for others to follow. We are often the first to venture onto new territory, like Rosa Parks, who sparked the civil rights movement, and Louise L. Hay, who overcame sexual abuse and cancer to write her first book "Heal Your Body" at 50 years of age, started Hay House publishing at 58, and helped gay men dying of AIDS in the '80s when most of society shunned them. Soul warriors help and defend those who cannot stand up for themselves, like children, animals, or adults undergoing a rough patch. The best example in the public aid and defense arena is Mother Teresa. She helped establish a leper colony, an orphanage, a nursing home, a family clinic, and a string of mobile health clinics.

I'm no Mother Teresa but I was given clear signs by the Universe that I am to follow the path of a healer. Of course, I asked for signs and validations because memories are wiped at birth, and I don't remember what I am meant to be doing. Many years ago, I asked the Universe to please show me a hummingbird feather if I was meant to do this work. A few weeks later, I saw a tiny feather at the bottom of the stairwell that leads to my apartment as my dog Peanut and I were on our way for our morning walk. At first, I couldn't believe that my eyes, which are terribly near-sighted, had spotted this teeny, tiny feather. Then, my brain couldn't logically believe that this was indeed a hummingbird feather. I then reissued an amended request to the Universe to show the feather coming right off the hummingbird's butt to confirm that I was meant to follow the path of a healer. A few weeks later, I was walking Peanut in the morning and as we were approaching home, I felt a hummingbird fly within a foot of my head and when I looked back to see where it came from, I found two hummingbird feathers floating gently down to the ground. Thank you, Universe! Your message has now been received! Up until that point, I had only waded ankle-deep into the healing profession, and that unequivocal sign led me to dive in, head first, with my full trust in the Universe. Since then, I've had the honor of helping hundreds of people in a variety of ways to clear something holding them back, get "unstuck," and most importantly, find their way back to their life's purpose and path. After the path has been cleared, we don't usually toot our own horns, and the people who take these new shortcuts carved out for them are usually so eager for movement after being "stuck" that they don't stop to ask or thank those who paved the way. All they know is there is now a path available to them that was not before, and that is enough for us light workers. The path leads to better health, abundance, happiness, faith, and fulfillment. Soul warriors aren't necessarily motivated by recognition. They are propelled by the notion of helping and uplifting others, creating positive change, and leaving the world a better place than how we found it.

Light workers are both teachers and healers but not necessarily in those specific occupations. Being a lightworker is who you are, not what you do. Due to the nature of who we are and our purpose here on Earth, our lives are often difficult and messy but we choose to be radiant and hold space for others using love and light. Our struggles and hardships are our opportunities for insight and healing, and it is our duty to pass along this wisdom and experience to others. We are encouraged by living our truth and our souls' purpose and are here to transform those who slumber who want to do the same. We use our spiritual discernment to illuminate the truth and stamp out the falsehoods. But even light warriors experience hard days filled with doubt and exhaustion—and this chapter is dedicated specifically to all of you to say—you are not alone on your journey. I see you. I've been you.

The good news is that, as we heal each of our hurts, traumas, egoic trips, and falls, we become better equipped to help others and more effective soul warriors. As a healer, I am always aware that before I can help others, I must first heal myself. I have personally experienced the pain of having an abusive father, being raped at 16 years old, having been cheated on by a boyfriend, having friends disconnect without reason, being ostracized for speaking my truth, and having mysterious foot issues. The foot issues were interesting because I would repeatedly tear tendons or ligaments or experience pain in my feet that podiatrists could not explain in my 30s. Louise Hay would say in her book, "You Can Heal Your Life", that it was a result of my fear of the future and of not stepping forward in life. In my childhood and young adulthood, I was a serious non-believer in what is now my intuitive practice, and I thought energy work was a load of rubbish. I was brought up in a Korean-American household that mocked energy work and intuition as illogical. After many years of unexplained pain in both my feet (the pain would alternate between both feet), I came to the conclusion that Universe wanted me to heal my feet, heal myself, embrace my intuition, and teach intuition and healing to others. My feet hurt because, spiritually, I dug my heels into my old position of resisting the call to light work and my true life purpose. I wanted no part of that, and by God, I went into it kicking and screaming, but finally, I did it, continue to do it, and of course, I haven't had problems with my feet since. I had to fully step into my role as a light worker and come to grips that I chose to be here to heal others. All of my experiences have helped me to help others who have experienced abuse, rape, infidelity, lack of abundance, weird friends, and even weirder health issues. I am immensely grateful for all that my pain has taught me. It feels like my life has been, up until now, about enduring hard experiences and then sharing my struggles in the hopes that it helps others. Some lessons are meant to be experienced firsthand, and others can be learned by learning the lessons of others. That's why we remember and teach our history to our children. In this case, all my pain provided valuable insight, but I always keep in mind that even as pain happens, suffering is optional.

Often, light workers live difficult and even painful lives. Like a butterfly, it is through struggle that we strengthen and heal ourselves and learn to spread our gorgeous wings to assist in the healing of others. We go through challenges and hardships because that is our initiation into the true transformation of becoming a light worker— first we learn to heal ourselves, and then we are able to heal and guide others. Our journey through challenges and hardships is instrumental in providing us with essential training. Over time, we gain wisdom from our experiences so that we may heal and guide others, or many times, we assist others in learning how to heal and guide themselves. Thus, the challenges and hardships we endure throughout our lives are not only blessings but also our sacred training ground.

As Martin Luther King, Jr. said, "Darkness cannot drive out darkness. Only light can do that."

Light energy is unlimited, expansive, positive, and loving. In contrast, dark energy feels heavy. Contrary to popular belief, darkness isn't always, nor does it come from, "evil." It comes from ego, is driven by fear, and can simply be things that cause pain or struggle like scarcity, feelings of emptiness, limitations, or isolation. Darkness seeks to manipulate and separate rather than connect and uplift. Because of this, darkness leads us away from our authentic and powerful selves. In order for soul warriors to transmute dark into light, they must experience darkness firsthand so they know how to recognize it and combat it, and this may often occur as if by trial and error. They may experience specific circumstances, short periods, and even long phases of darkness with the ones closest to them, like family and friends. They may have come into this life to resolve family generational trauma. Light workers also may have had a challenging childhood tinged with mental, emotional, or physical abuse. Soul warriors often attract people with problems because they need healing and are attracted to the soul warrior's light and healing energy. Conversely, the soul warrior is attracted to their need for healing, sometimes unknowingly if it is before they have come into the realization they are actually a light worker.

We've all heard the phrase, "No pain. No gain." For healers, my slogan is "My pain is your gain." Because I've dated narcissists, control freaks, energy vampires, "Peter Pan" types, and spineless jellyfish disguised as men, I can empathically help women and men who are having difficulties in relationships with these types of people. Because my father was verbally and physically abusive, people going through similar circumstances can more easily relate to me and vice versa. I have lived both a sheltered life under my overprotective parents and also found myself friends with drug addicts, prostitutes, gang members, and ex-cons. Because we, as human beings, experience both light and dark, our lives are constantly filled with dichotomy, practically on a daily basis. We may live alternating between high wattage light and dimming our light to the point of forgetting our purpose (to authentically "be" in our own power and brilliance). We may shine brightly in one area of life, like social dynamics and friendships, yet we stumble and second guess ourselves in love relationships. Financial difficulties may follow on one hand, but then you may also be an excellent at manifesting wealth at the eleventh hour. As we use our empathic abilities, our lives can be marked with great joy on the one hand, and on the other hand, we can empathically experience profound sadness or fear that is not even personally our own, as I did when the devastation of 9/11 occurred, or more recently when society was in a panic over Covid-19 and enraged over Black Lives Matter. As we help others find themselves and help set them on their life path, soul warriors can periodically also find themselves lost amidst the noise of the world.

Sometimes light workers are celebrated, however, more often than not, people either dismiss our work or fight against our offer of help because they are unable to see things in the same way that we can. In addition, people often harbor a great fear of the unknown and a huge resistance to change. On numerous occasions, I have had to stand my ground while well-intentioned people, seemingly in order to help, kindly lectured me that what I do is not sanctioned by God. I always gently respond by saying that God is the one who gave me my gifts of healing, intuition, and mediumship. I've also had to endure people who have said that it is immoral for me to charge my clients money for healing sessions. I don't try to counter this type of ignorance with hostile and aggressive action because I've learned that gentle words meant to sway have a better effect, much like how honey attracts more flies than vinegar. However, having to constantly neutralize fear and fend off people who, out of desperation, are physically or energetically draining can become exhausting. Over time, it can feel as though you are constantly trying to save someone from drowning, but over time, you run the risk of them pulling you down under and drowning with them. Additionally, seeing clients in crises, one after another, can be physically, mentally, and emotionally draining without breaks in between to process and celebrate the accomplishments, acknowledge how many clients you have healed, and how those healings have, in turn, healed you. I work a full-time job as a real estate paralegal during the day, and by night and weekends, I work full-time as a healer. While the numbers of people in need are many and I feel pressed to help as many people as possible, I realize that if I am working to the point of sickness or exhaustion, I cannot help anyone. Sometimes, as a healer, we have to fight our natural inclinations as "givers" to feel that taking time for yourself, in order to "live your best life" is selfish. I have yet to meet a soul warrior who hasn't experienced some form of exhaustion in their line of work as they so often try to do "everything" before they realize how important it is to try to find some balance in order to factor in their own mental, emotional, and physical health. I often teeter on the balance of racing to help as many people as I can and slowing down to learn and process my own lessons, celebrate the wins, and try my best to savor my life's journey along the way.

Soul Warriors use their light to be beacons of hope and guidance during good times and crises and to raise the vibration of the planet as a whole. Light workers turn their light on by following their internal guidance and callings of their souls. We recognize we are a part of something bigger than us, and there is a bigger plan for all of us in store within the Universe. We are here to serve humanity, but service doesn't mean we are always positive cheerleaders throwing glitter and fake smiles on terrible situations and calling on the power of rainbows. As we exude our light, we hold space for love and for others to thrive. For example, sometimes, just the simple act of listening and loving others despite themselves is the best source of healing. I cannot tell you how many times people I have just met have told me their deepest, darkest secrets, and the act of unloading has started the healing process. Just acknowledging and validating someone else's struggle and inner power, while confirming they are not alone, can be life changing. In this transaction of giving to others, we aren't always on the receiving end. As I said earlier in this chapter, I see you. You are celebrated. I acknowledge you for all you do without expecting praise but from a place of love and light.

Life should be expansive and full of fun, love, and laughs. At their best, light workers do not live in competition with anyone. Our spiritual awakening has instigated a desire to live a purposeful life of service in truth. We are truth seekers and truth warriors, and there is power and freedom that comes from living your truth. Light workers have a voice, and we are not afraid to use it because we possess the courage, conviction, and even the moral compulsion to stand up for what is right. Our self-awareness allows us to see the world differently, more clearly, and see the truth, even when others cannot. A soul warrior would be the lone voice in the crowd to cry out that "the emperor has no clothes," regardless of whether or not they would pay the price for their honesty. Falsehoods divide and isolate people and cause emotional cuts and injuries, so as a result, they prevent people from seeing and feeling their power. However, these are simply noise and distractions to chase people away from the truth, which is that the path to our own greatness is an inside job. There is no way to find peace outside of anything other than inside of ourselves. The truth sometimes just seems too simple.

As discussed, one of the common feelings resulting from fear is the feeling of isolation and separateness, and light workers often feel this way many times during their lives. To combat these feelings, building communities and personal support teams are so vital. By surrounding ourselves with other people who are positive and working toward similar life paths, we can learn from one another. Seasoned soul warriors can support the newly awakened light workers (of all ages) in all in different stages of the life game and warrior journey. By nature, light workers often need to do their growth work and trailblazing alone, but the dichotomy in this is that they are often plagued throughout their lives with the feeling that they don't truly belong anywhere. Additionally, people expect soul warriors to be in warrior mode and "on" all the time, and they expect you to tap in 24/7 when you are not technically working. But they may need to take longer to recharge their batteries or risk experiencing social anxiety and overload. This expectation of being "on" also leaves them with no one to talk to when they need connection and support. When I've had special experiences, I couldn't share them or my feelings with just anyone because I didn't think anyone would believe me. Years ago, when I was still new at using my gifts and in an intuition development class, the teacher asked me to tune into the master spirit guide of another student. I closed my eyes, and all I could see were red theater curtains that were closed, but I was aware of someone on the other side. I asked the person to reveal themselves, and there was a very long pause. Then I saw very long fingers pull one side of the curtains slightly apart to show an alien head with a flat top and long face with a big friendly smile. He showed just enough of himself through my third eye so as not to scare me. When I opened my physical eyes, I asked the teacher if the other student's guide was an alien, and she laughed heartily and said yes. What?! I didn't believe in aliens so my imagination couldn't have made this up. After the class, I tried to talk to someone to process, but I only had one friend at the time who was also an intuitive who could understand. All these situations can sometimes lead a light worker, especially a new one like me at that time, to feel flawed or broken and disconnected. However, even though I've grown and matured in my practice, now my schedule of working two full-time jobs often leaves no time for my friends, and I've seen my circle get smaller as friends get impatient and slowly start to fall off. It's hard to ask your friends not to take your lack of availability personally. I've also lost friends to jealousy even when I couldn't see the reason for their jealousy because I didn't believe my life was filled with anything that warranted being envious about.

I also want to stress that while it's important to share amongst other soul warriors, it's also important to realize that everyone's gifts are unique and individual. I say this so we don't limit ourselves by comparing our gifts and abilities to others and, even more so, to what others can and cannot do. When I was new to mediumship and taking development classes and circles, I was told that it was difficult to get the names of the deceased, and also it would take six months to contact the deceased after the date of passing. It turns out that was someone else's limitation that I took as gospel and assumed for myself. As a mediumship session with a client was about the end, my client threw out a name and asked about him. I tuned in and said he is in spirit and is taking responsibility for his passing. She started crying and told me that was correct and that he had passed away only days ago and that his memorial service was on the day I saw her. This reminded me that I had my first lesson about my own limitations (or lack thereof) on the first day I learned I had mediumship abilities. My best friend Brian had invited me on a trip to Lilydale, New York, and he signed us up for a Lisa Williams mediumship class once we were there, but I thought we were only in the class to watch her give readings. The audience was soon paired up for exercises, and I worked with the blond, middle-aged lady sitting next to me. After I shot Brian a look that said, "I'll kill you later for signing me up for this," I had to tune into any loved ones in spirit for this lady to complete the exercise. I had never done this before, so my first thought was to talk about opposites. She was blond with slightly wavy, mid-length hair and middle-aged, so I said I felt there was a young male with short, straight, dark hair about 20 years old and then proceeded to throw out more information, such as the young male loved motorcycles and died in a motorcycle related accident. I got his name is Matthew, but he didn't like to be called Matt. And I happily proceeded to "make up" more info. I just knew that my exercise partner would just shake her head and say she didn't have a clue what I was talking about. Instead, her eyes got big, and her jaw dropped, and said, "That's my son." What?! For many years after that, during mediumship trainings, I was told repeatedly that names are very difficult to get, so I struggled with getting names. One day, I was reminded by the Universe that I got a name on my first try that day in Lilydale. I had accepted a limitation that wasn't mine, and it is terribly difficult to unlearn something.

Soul warriors, although they may sometimes feel they don't always belong, are truly stronger when they work together and support each other. The "war" is not against each other, which is why it is so important that we do not fall into the trap of competing with one another. Every light worker has gifts, and we are all different, and therefore, we attract different people as clients. As Peter Parker's uncle said in Spiderman, "with great power comes great responsibility." Because of all of this, before I work with anyone, I spend a few minutes intentionally putting my ego aside, clearing karma, and then I begin to work on the client with a blank slate.

As light workers, we know at a very deep level that we must embrace both the peaks and the valleys of our journey through life because the valleys are just as important as the peaks. Light workers' lives are hardly ever graceful, uneventful, and pretty because the struggles and hardships of a soul warrior's life is a training ground that provides substantial room for growth and change, resulting in opportunities for greatness and reward beyond measure.

## About the Author

### YUSON SHIN

YuSon Shin is a healer, intuitive, medium, speaker, author and teacher of the healing and intuitive arts. She helps individuals heal themselves using past life, karma and ancestral clearing techniques utilizing the Akashic records and Chinese energy healing. She is also a practitioner of the Bengston Energy Healing Method, Reiki (Usui, Archangel & Kundalini), Integrated Energy Therapy, 5th Dimensional Quantum Healing, Quantum Touch, DNA Theta, and Access Bars. Her passion is teaching and helping people awaken their spiritual gifts and superpowers.

She is an author of "Holistic: 22 Expert Holistic Practitioners Help You Heal Mind Body and Spirit in New Ways" and "Manifestations: True Stories of Bringing the Imagined into Reality".

You can reach YuSon at YuSon@ShinHealingArts.com and get more information at www.ShinHealingArts.com.

NINETEEN

# Katie Carey

## CONNECTION TO ALL REALMS OF POSSIBILITY

Life was never plain sailing for me as a child. Born in the late 60s, I grew up in the 70s, where pain and suffering were all I ever witnessed around me. When my Dad became ill when I was five years old, I quickly became the girl who was going to change it all for my family. We were poverty-stricken, often went hungry, and no one seemed happy in our world. Unless my Dad and I were singing. We sang silly little songs together for as long as I could remember. We loved that. It was our thing. By the time I started school, I could already read and learn songs, and I was performing them in school, in the school playground, gathering an audience and making people feel better. How I loved it when they cheered and clapped and sang with me.

I had decided already that I was going to be a star and change my family's life one day soon. There were no other options. I could do that with my singing. My parents sometimes talked about the babies they had lost and how we wouldn't be here if that hadn't happened. We knew that we were very lucky to have been born at all. I look back now and see that they never did get over those traumatic losses —those tragedies. It was hard then for them to be good parents when it all began with such tragedy. They wrapped us up in cotton wool, never allowing us to play out or stay at friends' houses because I think they were really scared of losing us too.

I remember that my dad believed in spirit and reincarnation—and I remember him saying he had been to see a faith healer when I was very young. I had no idea what that was.

They used to leave us alone a lot. Quite bizarre, really, but people did that back then. They didn't trust other people to babysit for us. I remember deliberately flooding the kitchen floor and standing on a chair when my last babysitter came. She was so busy with her boyfriend that she was ignoring me—so I thought I would have some fun. Well, she was not allowed to come back after that.

I was nine years old when I first experienced being traumatised by death—three times in one year. It was 1977. I had lost my Nan, my dog was put to sleep, and Elvis Presley (who I had planned to sing with one day) died. Thankfully, when Nan died, I soon discovered that she wasn't really gone at all. At her funeral, I remember that I screamed—a real primal scream. I have only ever done that once since, when I lost my Dad. At Nan's funeral, I attempted to jump into her grave when they had lowered her coffin into the ground. I was even more upset when my family were all getting drunk after-wards, laughing and joking at her wake like nothing had happened. My Nanny was gone. How could they be happy? I didn't under-stand grown-ups!

I cried myself to sleep at night, so as not to upset my Dad, who then got angry, thinking I didn't care. I pleaded with God to let me please see my Nanny again. I spent all night with her in my dreams. She went on to visit me in my dreams regularly. That always made me happy. I felt that she was with me all of the time, just like God was. I didn't understand why they thought that God was at church. I felt him with me all the time. Yet, at Catholic Primary School, they always shamed us and made us feel bad when our parents wouldn't take us to church. I actually got to the stage later in life where I felt not worthy of being in a church.

I realised that this death thing wasn't really as bad as I thought it was. All I needed to do was ask Nan to help me, and she would be there, making me feel happy and strong again. By the time I got to secondary school, I was performing in big school shows and getting lead parts, even being seen and asked to audition for TV, radio, and theatre. People said that I was so talented. I was this four foot very small child with the voice of a woman. It was strange looking back. Now I think that maybe it was more about my presence and power on stage. I always had help with that. My Nan and anyone I knew in spirit would be there. I would call on them to help me to be the best I could be. This confidence was only available to me on stage though. I was terribly shy and didn't like attention in other ways. I was terrified of being me. This continued until I met my first husband, when I was told that my beliefs were crazy, that there was no such thing as God, and I was often put in my place when I said anything about my feelings. In fact, we never really did talk about feelings now I think about that, but we were both brought up not to.

A year after I got married, I had the first major evidence of spirit being real. That's how I interpret that experience now. I was 200 miles away from home, and suddenly on the bus, I felt a huge dark cloud over me and was crying so hysterically by the time I got to work …saying that my Grandad was dying. No one had told me this. I felt it deeply. Work helped me arrange the next train to Coventry. He died holding my hand within 10 minutes of me getting there. I believed my Nan led me there that day. Now I have spent decades studying the mind, spirit and mediumship, psychology, and Mental Health—I believe a combination of spirit, my intuition, and Grandad telepathically wanting to say goodbye to me, was the huge catalyst for my actions that day.

The next two years, I would go on to lose my other Grandad on the same date that my Nan had died. I didn't know what synchronicities were then, but I do now. My Dad passed on the summer solstice on June 21, 1993. It was the longest day, with him dying just before midnight. My husband had told me not to bother calling him back off of his course, if my dad died. He didn't want to be pulled out of his course. I spent that week with my Mum and my baby boy, who was just 13 months old. Strange things happened. Things would move and reappear. My Mum told me about things that she had seen after Dad died, and even her dog had seen something.

When I returned home a short while after Dad's funeral, I was woken in the night. We had a battery-operated toy radio in the bathroom. It began playing a song in the middle of the night. I went in half asleep and bleary eyed to turn it off. I saw that there were no batteries in it. That year, I had my first encounter with a psychic clairvoyant. He began singing songs to me. I was in tears because they were songs I had sang with my Dad. Or that he used to sing to me. This started my search for more knowledge about the spirit world.

Continuing on with my busy life, bringing up my children, moving home every year as my first husband was in the army, and then when I lived in my last military home, I went to a psychic party. I was literally mind blown. She brought my Grandad and my Dad through to me together. She gave me evidence that I knew was very real. Then, she asked me if this was my second marriage. When she saw the look on my face, she quickly changed the subject and told me that I would have a chance meeting with someone and my life would change direction.

I had kept that tape, and later, after going through a divorce from my first husband having married my second husband, I came across the tape again, and I realised that the telephone number on it was local. At this point, I had already trained in Mindfulness, Reiki, Psychic development and many holistic therapies and had discovered that husband number two was alcohol dependent. He was the reason I trained in all of those things. The little girl who had longed to save her Dad was now trying to save her sick Husband.

I called the psychic lady and she ended up being a volunteer for my charity. I set that up to help people in 2013 and ran it until I myself became too ill to hold everyone else up any longer. I became disabled. I believe now, from carrying the weight of everyone else's problems and avoiding looking at my own.

In 2020, my life changed. I turned to spirit in a big way. I recognised that I was a true soul warrior and that my soul had some serious impact that she wanted to make in the world. I got serious about meditation, about using the emotional freedom technique in my life to clear my subconscious patterns, programmes, and deep-seated beliefs that had been stuck in my body. I got interested in raising consciousness and the emotional intelligence of people in my world and connecting with my spirit family, and nature. I had decided that I would build the future that I wanted to live in, and I divorced my second husband and trained as a Moonologist, taking Moon cycles seriously too.

I had studied for a decade in personal and spiritual development, and it was time to step up into who I came here to be. My soul felt that calling so deeply, and I became so attuned to the right people, coaches, and opportunities to make that change happen. I now know that I will never disconnect myself from my connection to spirit and the higher realms. I trust myself and spirit more than I have ever trusted before. I know that plugged into my source, all things are possible. As humans, we fear death. Yet it comes to us all. We also have so much evidence of the afterlife. Yet it's brushed under the carpet as though it's a silly idea, and those who do believe are often ridiculed by those who don't.

99% of our reality is the unseen world. It is arrogant of us to think that all that there is, is what we see with our eyes. We're all here at this time for a reason. We all have access to our intuition and to our ancestor's support. I am proud to openly encourage that we do that, to empower ourselves and connect back into our true nature. Our innate wisdom and the abundance that the world truly has to offer us.

My life now consists of being more visible. Shining my light in podcast episodes and in books and sharing my story to normalise speaking our truth about matters and experiences of connection beyond the veil. It is my absolute honour to create books that give others a platform to do this. I now support metaphysical coaches and healers in offering them a place to share their stories, becoming bestselling authors in the process, and I offer them tools to shift their visibility blocks, increase their confidence, and shift feelings of over-whelm and imposter syndrome using the Emotional Freedom Tech-nique as part of my author VIP service. Bringing all of my knowledge and skills together. Serving the people that getting their stories and work taken seriously out in this world really matters too, at a time when we have a serious mental health epidemic that needs alternative solutions to those currently provided in society.

Many of my authors have joined my projects because they too access information and wisdom from beyond the veil, several of them have been psychic, and I have appeared in their world on dates that have meant something spiritually to them.

When we open our awareness to what's really possible, everything in our world can change, and personally, having lived in both worlds, I know which one I prefer. When I fully trust in a source of power that is far greater than me, amazing things keep happening.

A world where we know that our loved ones never really leave us, well, some may think that it's delusional, but it has always served me well, and I love the kind of people that have appeared in my world, who also live this way.

Life can feel easier with this level of trust and belief in the self and when you know that you are supported by spirit, no matter what you're going through. I know for a fact that when my spirit leaves this body, I will be intentionally supporting my family any way possible from the other side of the veil.

## About the Author

### KATIE CAREY

Katie Carey is the CEO of Soulful Valley Publishing, an International Best Selling Author and a globally ranked podcast host.

Katie is a passionate, creative, coach and mentor and loves helping metaphysical coaches and healers become more visible through her podcast and multi-author book opportunities.

Katie is a Reiki Master, EFT practitioner, Mindfulness and Law of Attraction Coach.

She has studied Psychology, Science of the Mind, Counselling & Psychotherapy and Challenging ideas in Mental health alongside Psychic Development, Mediumship and Angel therapy.

Katie won the Educational Spirit of Corby Award for the work she did with the Alternative Mental Health Charity that she founded.

Katie is a finalist in the 2021 Women's Business Award in the "Overcomer" category. She is disabled, being ill- health retired at 47 because of her conditions.

Katie lives in the UK and has 3 adult children and 2 grand-daughters.

https://www.soulfulvalley.com

TWENTY

# Veronika Gold

EN-JOY YOUR-SELF-EVOLUTION

Imagine a woman in her 30's with a huge heart overflowing with Love and understanding.

She feels Unity with ALL after a time of energetic separation from what she experienced in the past because she was learning how to "Love herself". She sees the bigger picture, even though she experienced emigration into a different continent than she was born. Despite all those self-destructive thoughts in the mind, despite all those self-destructive habits toward her body, childhood was based on arguments between parents (verbal fights between masculine and feminine figures). The environment created side effects on the lifestyle that could be healed. The past experiences didn't leave healthy models for relationships. She literally transformed all that childhood experience into a healing journey between her inner masculine (father) and feminine (mother) aspects of herself. To create a healthy relationship with herself.

~The same way as we relate to ourselves, we relate to others.~

That woman is ME.

The Unique journey of Body-Mind-Spirit has many forms. Especially when we have a look at how each unique individual has spiritual experiences on Earth. Earth is like school. There are teachers and students, and it is possible to experience some lessons. All that we go through is like a big book of Life. For me, it is like writing a book while I live my life, and simultaneously it is written into Akashic records.

Akasha is a place where all the past wisdom is stored across the whole time. In the 21st century, when we use social media, books, and a variety of platforms with our pictures, stories, and perspectives—literally speaking—all that information is becoming Akashic records in "matter".

My spiritual journey could be written as different aspects of me in one body. Those aspects of me have different personalities, they act differently, and they need different approaches to learn and thrive.

Overall, my evolutionary journey today is teaching me the most about how to balance inner masculine and feminine energies, so my inner child feels safe to express. Expression is part of the school of life, and I feel that there is a lot to be learned. Below is my spiritual journey presented in paragraphs—flow of life in words.

### Written by Inner masculine aspect of Veronika Gold

As a child, I have always been adventurous, creative, and authentic, and regardless of the setbacks that life has put across my journey, I have managed to keep them well alive throughout my existence. Those qualities make me feel at ease to engage with new experiences and reach out to other people and new environments. For me, the world is part of my comfort zone. Two areas that have been close to my heart since my first breath are music and singing. They are an intimate part of my soul's magic, which I became conscious of at an early age.

This spiritual awareness was already manifesting itself through a strong independent personality. At the age of six, I travelled on my own on a 15 minute train ride to go to school in a nearby town. I already had a sense of responsibility and accountability to be on time for both the train and school schedules. As extracurricular activities, I played the Soprano recorder for five years and practiced ballet for two years.

As the years passed by, my thirst for self-sufficiency grew even stronger, especially for music. At 11 years old, I decided to learn flute in Music school, where I studied recorder. With the abilities that I gained in focusing on routine and scheduling, there was a program of practicing the flute. At 18 years old, I won 1st place and a laureate prize in the duet Harflett (flute and harp) during the 2005 - 2006 Karel competition. In 2005 I joined the Amature Association of Youth, where I played in the Jistebnik orchestra for three years, traveling to Germany, Slovenia, and Italy. From 2006 up to 2011, I was part of the musical drama Woman from Bath, a production involving the cooperation of actress Marie Vikova.

I was very often part of some small or bigger group of artists. I feel more comfortable during performance—to be part of something bigger rather than a solo.

Despite my beautiful inner gifts that were so easy for me to express to the outside world, an unfulfilled expectation of my parents was still draining a lot of my energy within. In an attempt to address this ongoing issue with my father, I took a *"more pragmatic"* path by enrolling in a Hotel Industry and Tourism program. This deviation from my heart's lust for music only lasted a year, during which I gained out of the curriculum a deep understanding of customer service, including planning, organizing, and the importance of standards in a workplace. Those skills would come in handy later on in my life.

I promptly returned to the flute and harp duet and sang my heart out in choir. However, my dream of studying music in high school was first slowed down for one year since I only met the prerequisites of the talent exams the following year. Secondly, a part of me was still tormented by my parents' opposite expectations of what I should do with my life. To appease this inner conflict, I decided to travel back home every weekend to help my parents with household chores, including raising three younger siblings.

Being authentic to myself finally paid off as I reached in 2008 the Playing the flute - Level A from the Janeck Conservatory Ostrava. In 2010 I obtained, from the same institution, the Playing the flute - Higher National Diploma. As an extracurricular activity, I sang in the Komoraczech choir.

As my soul demanded more than just practicing and studying music, I started at 18 years old to share its magic with others by giving private recorder lessons. With my Higher National Diploma in hand, I took an entrepreneurial jump by co-founding a new musical school branch in Verovice where I was an active instructor for three years, teaching the flute, recorder, and music theory. I worked with individuals and groups as well as orchestras. I also gave guitar lessons for six months and piano lessons for one year.

It was during one of my orchestra trips in 2008 that I met my future husband and business partner in one person. With the family influence still having a disempowering effect on me, I decided to follow my husband to another part of the Czech Republic after he accepted a highly rewarding work opportunity. I then stopped music altogether and got pregnant.

I gave birth to a wonderful boy in spring 2014. After some serious considerations, my husband and I decided to immigrate to Canada in April 2015 and settled down in Kitchener, Ontario.

For two years I stayed at home to take care of my son, after which I joined a home cleaning company for one year. Following my excellent work performance, I took on new responsibilities from training new employees, pay slips, and customer services. I considered becoming a business partner with my boss, and then out of the blue, I felt a strong need to serve others. A call of the spirit to help kids by fostering three children from newborn to age five. Following this half-year experience, I offered my services as a nanny.

Meanwhile, my husband had started a home business, Somavedic Canada, a distributor of Somavedic, a cutting-edge energy cleansing device. We had bought our first one in the Czech Republic, and the effects that we experienced were so empowering that we decided to contact the inventor and offer him our services to import and distribute his products across Canada. Since I needed a change from my nanny job, I took the opportunity to join as a partner.

With most of the literature about Somavedic in Czech, everything from marketing to educational material had to be translated and developed according to the Canadian market and all this on top of the regular e-commerce activities such as customers' inquiries, supply chain management, and distribution that I was taking care of. With the growing wonder of the general public about the 5G network, we also spend a lot of energy to educate the people about the benefits of Somavedic to counter the potential disempowering effects of this high-frequency network, including geopathogenic stress. Somavedic Medic Green ultra amplified energies around my awakening and helped me open my heart and seek my own truth. It is based on crystals, so Somavedic itself is a living entity in a home place ( those who feel energies will understand this phrase), and it supported my intuition generously. Even when I added Somavedic Gold as an energy helper to clean my deep ancestral past, I sometimes wonder how far I would get without energetic support of higher frequency being as an element of gold does for humans.

To make ends meet at the beginning of the Somavedic business venture, I decided to go back to house cleaning but this time to work for my own by starting Veronika Gold Cleaning Services.

Simultaneously while I did cleaning jobs for people, I played as a busker at Kitchener Market or St. Jacobs farmers market.

In those times I travelled a lot around. I visited Algonquin, Bon Echo, and Killarney. The most transformative vacation happened in Newfoundland province (summer 2018). I was facing the significant feeling of separation from my husband, family, and myself. I felt so alone, despite the fact, I was traveling with family members in Newfoundland island.

On top of all those feelings, I asked for a spiritual divorce in spring 2019. I neutralized promises that I gave to my husband in church, and we became best friends who support each other when we need to.

I have started with my deep self-healing journey through intimacy and physical alchemy.

Deeper—I discovered who I am the more connected I became with nature, the metaphysical world, and the esoteric world on a conscious level. Years ago, I followed intuition without questioning or analyzing too much. For me to become conscious about the esoteric world and use it in my favour was a shifting experience.

I am starting to feel how my feminine is getting more to the fore-front, so I will continue as my inner feminine aspect of me.

## Written by Inner feminine aspect of Veronika Gold

The life after spring 2019

My spiritual awakening comes to me in waves. And each wave brings something new and exciting even though some of the waves are so strong that to surf on them takes a lot of sense for balance to keep on top.

After a spiritual divorce with my husband, I experienced spiritual romance with a few people.

If someone asked me what I experienced, I would say I am evolving. I wasn't dating.

What I experienced during those months was very typically named as awakening in its most potent form. Alchemy between men and women might have a variety of side effects.

I had difficulties with sleeping, and I was overflowing with energy. I experienced energies between ecstatic days to the most fearful feelings that could be experienced in human form.

This emotional alchemy opened my sense for psychic abilities, sense for channeling, sense for opening heart, sense for creativity, sense for deep awakening toward "who am I".

Side effects of making love between two individuals can bring the best and the worst of you to the surface.

When both parts of the couple are willing to be fully open for communication and practise of being present, the transformative magic can happen even without any outside forces. And, of course, it is necessary to have consensual energy to play with. Consent is very important in the energetic world to create with grace.

In that time, I did a hypnotherapy course, and with a combination of physically making love, it activated my connection with The Intuition. I understood the empath's qualities of myself—reading angel numbers became second nature, synchronicities amplified after physical alchemy, and I had become one with nature spontaneously. The outcome of such an experience was, for example, a deep connection with water. I was standing in a lake, and I understood water and waves. I understood water language and how it is talking to me. Or on different days, I was walking in the forest, and I became one with the forest and environment I was in. I united with ALL THERE IS.

Physical intimate connection was teaching me how to deeply open and surrender into masculine energy.

I used a hypnotic state for my meditative practise, so I deepened my body experiences. It was for me to train myself to be in the present moment, rather than wonder in the past or future.

I was learning how to follow the wisdom of my menstrual cycle and moon cycle. The main way I receive information from above is through feelings—to do, to act, to create, to follow.

Reading those feelings/energy uploads is my ongoing process of learning, so I can serve more efficiently and read energies with punctuality.

Recommendation: Surround yourself with some modality that influences you deeply daily. I chose Somavedic and later Kangen water with a combination of breathing techniques. We are 70% water. It means H2O. Hydrogen and oxygen. You can change yourself from 70% just by how you take care of yourself.

I wouldn't even name myself as Lightworker. I feel more like a Lighthouse—standing, waiting, showing direction.

Even my role to be a healer would be written as someone who faced pain and suffering and found itself staring right back. Healers who create themselves through all of the adversity, and in the process, inspire others to do the same.

Everyone heals themselves. My viewpoint is to inspire others to do the same.

The most important growth doesn't happen when I do meditation or sit in nature.

It happens in the midst of conflict between my inner feminine and inner masculine aspect of me. When I feel doubts, angry, scared, or repeating old patterns on and on, and then I suddenly realize that I have a choice to act upon that differently.

In the last two years, I have completed the following courses; Reiki Master; the Professional Hypnosis Certification; the Past Life Exploration Certification; and the Life Between Lifetimes Certifications. I supported my touch sense through learning Bowen therapy and Four-wheel consent, which has been teaching me the Art of giving and receiving. My studying continued with the breathwork Energy codes facilitator program, and here I am now. Writing chapter into the Soul Warrior book to imprint into "matter" part of my life experience.

All those modalities served me on my path to awaken my senses and understand my unique path from a deeper perspective. Regarding all of those courses, my self-healing is an ongoing business anyway. My higher self has some plan with me. I don't know what is next, but in the right time and place, it is going to be revealed to me through my intuition.

What is the disadvantage of too much open intuitive sense?

I am constantly receiving a variety of energies (or let's call them information) from around. The most important part for me is to ground in such situations. When the collective goes through deep transformational processes, I feel them even though it is happening on the opposite side of the world. It depends on how strong energy is and if there was some connection with that place through my ancestral past. From another point of view, when someone struggles with something, my best-discovered action is just holding space for that situation. Yes, I receive a quantum of follow-up information during or after, which overwhelms my energy system. Still, again, the point is to ground that energy and re-share whatever feels the best in that moment. Because, believe me or not, it feels like I would explode if I wouldn't share that stream of energy coming through me. And my spiritual ego is very often giving me an opportunity to grow because the constant feeling of not good enough, not done enough, not finished enough is coming very often to me on my path. It often feels like above me is a very huge source of not embraced energy that is awaiting me to be embodied in physical form.

Energy waits to be embodied. In other words, the unhealed past is coming to the surface to be acknowledged, transformed, and transmuted into "Love".

How to ground?

Step on the ground barefoot, focusing on breath or flame gazing, play your favourite song, do your favourite physical exercise, create art.

Dancing, humming, singing, bringing your attention into the body.

## *Written by Inner child aspect of Veronika Gold*

Write a letter to your inner child. Prepare pen and paper in front of you. Find a comfortable place where you can be with yourself and close your eyes.

Take three deep breaths.

Open your eyes and start writing a letter from your inner child to your current version of self. Write with your non-dominant hand. If you are left-handed, use your right hand to write this inner child letter. If you are right-handed, use your left hand to write. Do not rush the process of writing. Reconnect fully with your inner child and let that child talk to you.

What would your inner child write to you? Do you need to work on something that your inner child shared with you? Are you willing to help your inner child to have harmonized inner feminine and masculine energy so the internal child can feel supported and loved by her parents?

En-JOY YOUR-self-Evolution

P.S.
What would you leave here on the planet for tomorrow?

## About the Author

### VERONIKA GOLD

Veronika Gold is the healer and artist with passion for music and wisdom. Her skills of intuitive healing and devotion for evolution creates ripple effects in the energy field which transforms many.

Her ability to spontaneously improvise with music brings energies on the planet and heals her. Once her gifts with talents and creations are shared, it heals others as well.

Veronika has studied earthly skills such as: Music school, Hypnotherapy, Bowen therapy, Energy codes and becoming a Reiki Master. On her earthly journey she plays roles of student, teacher, friend, mother, lover, helper, business partner, entrepreneur, artist, improvizator, embodied feminine, inner child support maker and masculine embracer.

Her passion for nature and environment inspired her to continue using zero waste strategies at home, sustainable living with quality filtered and energised water, including a feng shui environment— harmonized by Somavedic. How she cares about her Body-Mind-Spirit is inspirational for her clients and friends.

En-JOY YOUR-self-Evolution
info@veronikagold.fun
Website: www.veronikagold.fun
Youtube channel: https://www.youtube.com/.../
UCs0WcGrQwms8dbYXnaA-u7Q/videos

Instagram: https://www.instagram.com/enjoy.yourself.evolution/
LinkTree: https://linktr.ee/enjoy.yourself.evolution

TWENTY-ONE

# About the Publisher

## HOUSE OF INDIGO

House of Indigo, is a multi-media publishing company that supports conscious and soul-led entrepreneurs and practitioners through the creation of books, oracle decks and more.

Through liberating our personal stories, we are able to create a bigger impact and positively influence the world.

Our mission is to elevate the authority and showcase the expertise of outstanding and integrous professionals with similar personal values to create massive collective change.

We believe collaboration propels everyone forward and is the way of the future.

You have a unique imprint in the world, illuminate it.

For inquires on publishing, speaking, upcoming retreats or writing courses, please contact us at:

House-indigo.com
publishing@jessverrill.com

Made in United States
North Haven, CT
15 November 2021

11135991R00142